JUNGLE DOCTOR'S
Crooked Dealings

④

JUNGLE DOCTOR'S
Crooked Dealings

Paul White

CF4•K

10 9 8 7 6 5 4 3 2

Jungle Doctor's Crooked Dealings, ISBN 978-1-84550-299-7
© Copyright 1988 Paul White
First published in 1959, reprinted in 1965, 1968
Paperback edition 1975, revised 1988
by Paul White Productions
4/1-5 Busaco Road, Marsfield, NSW 2122, Australia

Published in 2007 and reprinted in 2008 by
Christian Focus Publications, Geanies House, Fearn, Tain,
Ross-shire, IV20 1TW, Scotland, U.K.
Fact files: © Copyright Christian Focus Publications

Cover design by Daniel van Straaten
Cover illustrations by Craig Howarth
Interior illustrations by Graham Wade
Printed and bound in Denmark by Norhaven A/S

Since the Jungle Doctor books were first published there have been a number of Jungle Doctors working in Mvumi Hospital, Tanzania, East Africa - some Australian, some British, a West Indian and a number of East African Jungle Doctors to name but a few.

African words are used throughout the book, but explained at least once within the text. A glossary of the more important words is included at the front along with a key character index.

CONTENTS

Fact File: Paul White

Born in 1910 in Bowral, New South Wales, Australia, Paul had Africa in his blood for as long as he could remember. His father captured his imagination with stories of his experiences in the Boer War which left an indelible impression. His father died of meningitis in army camp in 1915 and he was left an only child without his father at five years of age. He inherited his father's storytelling gift along with a mischievous sense of humour.

He committed his life to Christ as a sixteen-year-old school-boy and studied medicine as the next step towards missionary work in Africa. Paul and his wife, Mary, left Sydney, with their small son, David, for Tanganyika in 1938. He always thought of this as his life's work but Mary's severe illness forced their early return to Sydney in 1941. Their daughter, Rosemary, was born while they were overseas.

Within weeks of landing in Sydney Paul was invited to begin a weekly radio broadcast which spread throughout Australia as the Jungle Doctor Broadcasts - the last of these was aired in 1985. The weekly scripts for these programmes became the raw material for the Jungle Doctor hospital stories - a series of twenty books.

Paul always said he preferred life to be a 'mixed grill' and so it was: writing, working as a Rheumatologist, public speaking, involvement with many Christian organisations, adapting the fable stories into multiple forms (comic books, audio cassettes, filmstrips), radio and television, sharing his love of birds with others by producing bird song cassettes - and much more...

The books in part or whole have been translated into 107 languages.

Paul saw that although his plan to work in Africa for life was turned on its head, in God's better planning he was able to reach more people by coming home than by staying. It was a great joy to meet people over the years who told him they were on their way overseas to work in mission because of the books.

Paul's wife, Mary, died after a long illness in 1970. He married Ruth and they had the joy of working together on many new projects. He died in 1992 but the stories and fables continue to attract an enthusiastic readership of all ages.

Fact file: Tanzania

The Jungle Doctor books are based on Paul White's missionary experiences in Tanzania. Today many countries in Africa have gained their independence. This has resulted in a series of name changes. Tanganyika is one such country that has now changed its name to Tanzania.

The name Tanganyika is no longer used formally for the territory. Instead the name Tanganyika is used almost exclusively to mean the lake.

During World War I, what was then Tanganyika came under British military rule. On December 9, 1961 it became independent. In 1964, it joined with the islands of Zanzibar to form the United Republic of Tanganyika and Zanzibar, changed later in the year to the United Republic of Tanzania.

It is not only its name that has changed, this area of Africa has gone through many changes since the Jungle Doctor books were first written. Africa itself has changed. Many of the same diseases raise their heads, but treatments have advanced. However new diseases come to take their place and the work goes on.

Missions throughout Africa are often now run by African Christians and not solely by foreign nationals. There are still the same problems to overcome however. The message of the gospel thankfully never changes and brings hope to those who listen and obey. *The Jungle Doctor* books are about this work to bring health and wellbeing to Africa as well as the good news of Jesus Christ and salvation.

Fact File: Bilharzia

One disease that is common throughout sub-Saharan Africa is bilharzia.

Bilharzia mainly affects people in developing countries. People who bathe in lakes, rivers, canals or in freshwater pools that haven't been chlorinated in the tropics are at risk of developing bilharzia. People from the UK become infected only when visiting tropical countries. It's more common in children. Over one billion humans are at risk worldwide and approximately 300 million are infected.

The disease is carried in many of Africa's fresh waterways. Bilharzia is spread by a tiny, waterborne parasite. These worm like creatures are at first carried by water-snails, but eventually leave these snails in order to burrow into human skin. Once within a human body they multiply in the bloodstream and then work their way to the walls of the intestine or bladder, where they begin to lay eggs.

The best way to avoid infection is not to swim in dams and rivers where possible. Although the snails favour sheltered areas you still may contract the disease in faster waterways.

Once infected people may not feel very ill at first, and perhaps all they will be aware of is a feeling of ill health. However, once the infection is established, abdominal pain is common. Fortunately, bilharzia is easily and effectively treated with the right medicine. No vaccine is available.

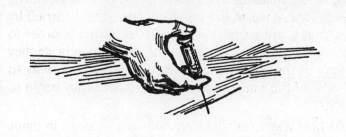

Fact File: Characters

Let's find out about the people in the story before we start. Bwana is the Chief Doctor and the one telling the stories. Daudi is his assistant. Take a moment or two now to familiarise yourself with the names of the people you will meet in this book.

Baruti – hunter
Bwana – chief doctor
Bwana Chigoda – carver
Chuma – blacksmith
Daudi - assistant
Goha – boy with deformed face
Isaka – Son of the Chief
Mboga – hospital worker
Mdimi – boy attacked by a lion
Nusu – had a twisted face
Perisi - nurse
Punda – the donkey
Seko – Goha's little dog
Wendwa - night nurse
Woga – the singer

Fact File: Words

EXPRESSIONS THAT ADD EMPHASIS:
Eheh, Heh, Hongo, Kah, Koh, Kumbe, Ngheeh, Yoh

SENTENCES:
Zo gono? - How did you sleep?
Ale zo gono gwegwe? - How did you sleep?

WORDS

Asante - thank you

Basi – enough

Debiful – kerosene tin full

Dudus – germs or insects

Fez - hat

Fundi - an expert

Gazette – newspaper

Habari? – What is the news?

Habari njema - The news is good

Hodi? - may I come in?

Ilimba – musical instrument

Ipu - swelling

Jambo - How are you?

Kabisa – completely

Kanzu – long garment

Karibu - Come in

Kiboko - the hippo

Lulu baha - straight away

Machisi - devils

Magu - I don't know

Mbisi - the hyaena

Mbukwa - good day

Muganga - a medicine man

Mzee - Elder of the Tribe

Mzuri - I'm fine

Ngubi - the wart hog

Nhembo - the elephant

Panga - knife

Pombe - beer

Sindano - the needle

Singila – musical instrument

Taka taka - the rubbish

Twa - full to the neck

Vidudu - germs

Wuvimbo - a swelling

Zaburi - The Psalms

TANZANIAN LANGUAGES: Swahili (main language)
Chigogo (one of the 150 tribal languages)

1
Hunchback of the Jungle

The flames of the camp fire threw huge shadows on the walls of the jungle hospital.

From the dispensary door I could see young Goha. He stood in the background, but his deformed face and the unsightly lumps on his back were clearly visible.

Daudi whispered, 'How long before we can do his operations, Bwana?'

'Everything depends on how he responds to the new medicines. Mosquitoes have done much harm to his blood.'

Lying at Goha's feet was Seko, his small dog, who seemed to have the ability to smile.

Daudi gripped my elbow. 'Look at that dog, doctor.'

Seko's ears were flat. He trembled all over.

'Seko, come here!' ordered Goha, but instead of obeying the dog tried to creep under a three-legged stool.

Goha put one hand over the twisted side of his face and moved forward to pick up the little animal.

It all happened in a second. A brown, hunched-up shadow came rocketing out of the darkness. Snarling, it grabbed the small dog by the scruff of the neck and shot off again into the gloom of the night.

Daudi jumped to his feet. '*Mbisi* - the hyaena! Quickly, after the brute!'

I snatched up my torch. Its beam followed the sound of the little dog's howling as I swept the corn garden systematically with light.

'Save him, Bwana!' gasped Goha as we dashed through the gate.

A muffled howl came from the path ahead as the

beam of light picked out the hyaena trying to swerve round a tall man carrying a knobbed stick.

Thump! The club whacked into the jungle scavenger's ribs. A second wallop caught the hyaena where his tail joined his hunched back. With a yelp he disappeared in the direction of the jungle.

Goha picked up the small dog, who lay huddled beside the path. He ran back and gently put him into my arms. Tears ran down Goha's face.

I examined the dog. One leg was broken, and the teeth of the hyaena had torn him savagely.

In an undertone I said to my medical assistant, 'Daudi, he is so badly hurt that the kindest thing to do would be to help him join his ancestors.'

'*Eheh*,' he agreed.

Goha stood up and came towards me. There was a tragic look on his small face. The sweat on his forehead stood out in beads. 'Bwana, you won't let Seko die?'

'It might be kinder if we saved him from suffering.'

'Seko's brave, Bwana. Please save his life.'

'I'll do what I can. Mboga, take Goha and see that he rests quietly in bed.'

The male nurse smiled. 'Yes, Bwana.'

I put my hand on the boy's shoulder. 'I'll operate, and when we're finished I'll tell you all about it.'

The sick boy looked longingly at his dog, who made a feeble effort to lick his hand.

'We will need penicillin to save Seko,' said Daudi anxiously, 'but in a hospital like this where we are always short of drugs, what can we do?'

'Bwana,' urged Mboga, 'the dog means much to the boy. If Seko dies, Goha will fret. We're not just fighting for the dog's life. Let's do all we can.'

'We will, but I've only operated on a dog once before.'

'*Kah*!' muttered Daudi as he started the primus stove. 'It is a new work, boiling up instruments for an operation on a dog.'

I injected anaesthetic into the little creature, scrubbed up my hands, and set to work.

It was complicated surgery. After an hour Seko, heavily bandaged and with one leg in plaster, lay in a padded box. Mboga carried the small dog to the ward where the glimmer of a lantern showed that Goha was still awake.

Daudi went in. 'The Bwana worked with skill. His hand was as gentle for the dog as it will be for you.'

'*Eheh*,' nodded Goha, 'of course.'

'He also gave injections of penicillin, for the teeth of hyaena are covered with *vidudu* - germs.'

The boy asked hoarsely, 'Bwana, what is news of my dog?'

'He's sick, very sick. Do you want me to tell you exactly what I think?' He nodded. 'The chance for him to recover is small.'

Tears rolled down his face. 'Bwana, you did everything you could?'

'Yes, everything.'

He lay there quietly for a while and then, 'Does God listen when we pray for dogs?'

'Yes, Goha, he does. But we can't tell God what to do. He knows best. Often he is answering before we ask. You see, there would have been no hope for Seko unless that tall man with the knobbed stick had been on the path. Also, he would certainly have died if we hadn't operated at once. It isn't only a matter of his neck and leg, but the teeth of hyaena have torn him deeply inside.'

'What have you done, Bwana?'

'I have fixed everything up, but it was not easy. I have also set and splinted his left leg. It was not only broken but it was crushed. Seko will have much pain.'

'Bwana, for a year Seko has been my only friend.'

'We know these things, Goha, so we have done the best we could.'

The boy climbed out of bed and quietly knelt down.

2
The Man with the Twisted Face

The drums throbbed in the village as I walked under the pepper trees. A hand came out of the darkness. Startled I swung round, and a deep voice boomed, 'Bwana, it is I, Nusu, who have come to greet you.'

I held up my hurricane lantern and peered into a face half covered by a huge hand.

'Remember me, Bwana?'

'*Kah*! How could I forget the man with the twisted face?'

He laughed and removed his hand to show a broad smile on a normal face.

'I came to greet you, Bwana, but a hyaena with a dog in its mouth ran into my leg. I thumped it with my knobbed stick.'

'*Yoh*, Nusu, you have done an important thing for a boy and his dog. You, and only you, can help him in another special matter. Tomorrow will you come at the time of the morning drum?'

At dawn an urgent voice sounded outside the mosquito-proof wire of the window of my bedroom.

'Bwana!'

'What's up?'

I recognised the voice of Wendwa, the night nurse. 'It's young Goha. His temperature is 41°.'

'I'll come at once.'

I dressed rapidly and ran with my mind asking, what could have caused that wild rise?

I tiptoed into the ward and took Goha's pulse. It was normal. His forehead was cool.

'Let me see the thermometer, Wendwa.'

It read 41°, but the mercury wouldn't shake down. She raised her eyebrows.

'Let's try another one.' I checked it, put it under Goha's arm and kept it there for three minutes.

His temperature was 37° - perfectly and beautifully normal.

'Bwana,' whispered the night nurse, 'I'm sorry. I thought you ought to know at once. I didn't wait to try another thermometer.'

'You were right. I'm only thankful he doesn't have a high fever like that. While I'm here, how's that small dog?'

'Asleep, Bwana.'

Daudi appeared in the doorway. 'What's happening, doctor?'

'A false alarm. I was told Goha's temperature was way up but it was only the thermometer that had fever, not the boy.'

Daudi grinned. 'How's the smiling dog?'

We hardly dared to look into the box where he lay. When we did, two brown eyes looked up and a curly tail wagged feebly.

'He's alive and better than seemed possible,' I breathed. Goha awoke and eagerly bent down to look at his dog. His eyes were glistening. 'Bwana, Seko's much better.'

'*Yoh!*' agreed Daudi. 'Surely it is a thing of thankfulness about the little dog.'

Goha broke in. 'Off and on all night I have been asking God to help him.'

'Would it not be good now to thank him?'

We did.

A drum started to beat.

'*Yoh*,' smiled Daudi as Nusu joined us. 'An old friend has arrived. And you, Mboga have a story of high interest for Goha.'

'Truly. I had just started working at the hospital two years ago and Nusu came with a banana leaf covering half his face. With this in place he looked normal. But when you saw the other side, *koh*! How twisted it was. His eye was lower on the right side than the left and the corner of his mouth seemed to go up and meet it.'

Goha spoke softly, '*Kumbe*! You were almost as I am?'

They stood looking at each other for a while then both smiled. The boy's face was distorted.

'*Yoh*, Great One, the Bwana worked well on your face.'

'*Eheh*! He will do the same for you also.'

Goha started to ask questions. I left them talking together.

As we worked that afternoon, Daudi pointed to Goha and Nusu sitting under the buyu tree. 'There is good work going on there, doctor. That Nusu has truly become one of God's family. *Hongo*, my heart feels warm to hear him tell what is happening in his life.'

'Truly, Daudi. I'm looking forward to hearing him tell his story tonight.'

A little while after sunset, I heard cheerful singing round the camp fire as I visited the ward. Seko was certainly holding his own. Goha, as usual, had half his face covered with his hand.

'Come with me, Goha, and join the singing.'

As we sat by the fire, Nusu took up his drum and we sang one of the tribal responsive songs.

'Tell us about your trouble and its cure now, Nusu.'

'*Eheh*, Bwana.' He stirred up the fire. 'Behold, I had heard many stories of the work of your medicine here. There was a child who had a large ulcer on her face and you cured it, and then an old man who had no joy in his stomach. *Kumbe*, you treated it with success and he sang your praises strongly. It was a thing of wonder in our village. I heard these words and many more, Bwana, while I sat in the darkness of my house, for I feared to go outside.

'I came at night, for there was no joy in eyes that looked curiously at me. You examined me and asked many questions. Then you said, "*Kumbe*! I can fix that up for you. In a moment I will get a bandage and cover that side of your face."

'Your words brought small joy, for covering my face did not cure the trouble. But you were the doctor so I agreed and Wendwa put on a bandage. I looked at myself in the mirror. *Yoh*! If only both sides had looked like that!'

'Wait a bit, Nusu,' I interrupted. 'Before you went home that evening I called Daudi and Wendwa aside. You know our habit here each day is to ask God to guide us in all we do. We prayed together and then I told them, "This man's case is beyond me. I have never seen anyone like him. I'm not sure what the cause of his trouble is. Let us ask God to help because it says in the book written by James, "If any of you lacks wisdom let him ask God."

'Later I took through my surgical books with care. For hours I read, and when I put the last one back on the shelf I still had no idea what to do.'

'Had you no more books, Bwana?' asked Goha.

'None, but on the table was a copy of the Medical Journal that had arrived in the mail that afternoon. I tore off the wrapping and turned over the pages. Suddenly my eyes opened wide. There was an article on the very thing I was looking for. There in front of me was a picture of a man exactly like you, Nusu. Underneath the photo were all the details of how to do that operation. But this was small comfort, for it said clearly that it was only to be undertaken by the experienced.'

Daudi took up the tale. '*Kumbe*, doctor! To those of us who help you it was a thing of wonder, and Nusu here drew in his breath to see the pictures in that journal.'

Nusu laughed. 'Bwana, if your face had been twisted like mine you would have had deep interest, too, in that *gazetti* with its photographs.'

'*Hongo*, Nusu! Your eyes really stuck out when I showed you those before and after pictures. But you

26

remember I explained that it was no easy task ahead of us. We were ready to do our best but couldn't be sure that the result would be all that you expected or we hoped.'

'Bwana, I put myself in your hands.'

Daudi broke in. 'That was faith. The doctor told you that perhaps he could help. Surely we do a much safer thing when we put our lives into God's hands. Did not Jesus say, "Come unto me and I will give you rest?" There's nothing of the perhaps about that.'

Nusu smiled. 'It took me a while to understand that, but I do now. The night before you worked I had many doubts. Sleep was hard to catch, but Daudi came with a yellow pill and at dawn you operated.'

'Wait a bit, Nusu. How do you think the doctor feels the night before?'

'*Magu* - I don't know.'

'I felt unhappy. The work was beyond me so I turned over the pages of my Bible and found the words, "I the Lord God will be your confidence". That made me feel better about the operation.'

Nusu nodded.

'What I was looking for was a little piece of gristly tissue that was growing in the wrong place and pulling both your eye and mouth out of place. It was no easy work to do. Anyway, after about half-an-hour, from underneath your eye I removed a swelling the size of the last joint of my thumb. It was tucked away and stuck down deep to the skin and bone, anchoring each in an unnatural position. The last few minutes were really thrilling for Daudi and myself.'

'Words of truth,' broke in my assistant. 'They were, for as the tumour came out you could see the side of his face coming back into place. The twists disappeared, the mouth straightened and the eye, *yoh*, it was suddenly normal.'

Nusu laughed. 'But, Bwana, how I rejoiced when you asked for a mirror to be brought.'

Wendwa smiled. 'It was one of the things I will never forget, that moment when you first looked into that mirror.'

Nusu shook his head. 'It was quite beyond wonder. My tongue could grasp no words but my heart sang with joy. Bwana, no one could have done more for anyone than you have done for me. You have made my crooked places straight again. *Eeeh*!

'You showed me the small lump of stuff that was the cause of all the trouble. It was a worthless small thing. *Kah*! I rejoiced when I saw it go into the rubbish bin.'

'Suppose, Nusu, that we'd left that bandage over your face. It would have hidden your trouble. No one would have noticed and everyone would have said how neat the bandage looked.'

'But, you would not have removed the cause. My trouble would have remained. Also, to use both eyes and all your mouth is much better than only half.' He smiled an almost straight smile. 'You explained this to me carefully and simply. You said that it was this swelling that made my face crooked, that made my life miserable and that made me frightened. You told me sin was like this, for sin twists, brings fear and misery and death.

'*Kumbe*, I understood. It was no good covering sin up. I had to come to the only One who could help to get rid of it. He is Jesus Christ, the Son of God.'

Daudi smiled. 'Jesus certainly took from your heart the sin that damages and twists. He forgave you. Behold, it was small hardship to the Bwana, nor did it cause him pain to remove your trouble. For Jesus it was altogether different and this is what God says about it, "Although he was the Son of God and equal with God, he put aside his divine glory and became human like you and me and lived humbly and appeared as a man amongst men. He was so obedient to God that he went to the point of giving up his life by dying like a criminal on the cross." And he did all this so that you and I might get rid of the twisting of sin from our lives.'

'*Kah*,' said Nusu. 'My life is different now, Bwana. People can look at me without shuddering and I have no shame and sorrow in my heart.'

Wistfully Goha looked across at me and said, 'Hope grows within me.'

3

Tangles Start

Goha sat under a pepper tree with Seko crouched at his feet. The boy gripped my arm.

'Behold, Seko's wounds heal fast, Bwana.'

'They do indeed. Dogs recover more quickly than people.' I handed him a *panga*. 'Will you take this jungle knife and cut me six strips of fine twisty vine, as thin as string but very strong?'

Goha nodded. 'How long, Bwana?'

'*Ooooh*, about twice as long as your arm.'

'*Eheh*, what are they for?'

'They are food for your understanding – a splint for your memory.'

The African boy looked down at his dog, who was beginning to hobble round on three legs, the fourth being firmly in a plaster splint. '*Yoh*, Seko, the Bwana surely talks in riddles.'

An hour later Goha was back at the door. '*Hodi* – may I come in?'

'*Karibu*! Come in!'

He tilted his head on one side. 'Bwana, you sent me to the jungle to cut these bits of vine.'

'Look at them and describe them to me.'

'Bwana, they are green, thin, strong and curly.'

I grasped a strip of vine by each end, drawing my hands further and further apart. The vine straightened.

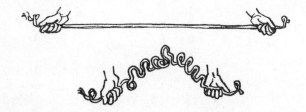

'And now, Goha?'

'Bwana, it's as straight as a taut rope, but only because you hold it apart with strength.'

'If I let it go?'

'It will twist up again, for it is the nature of vines to do that.'

'Truly. You said exactly what I wanted you to say. In the same way it is the nature of men to be twisty in their doings. Evil does that to people. It is one of the ways you can recognise sin.'

'*Eheh*, Bwana, like the track of a snake in the dust?'

'Truly. One of the reasons Jesus came to earth was to make the crooked places straight. It is our job to help him. This is how we show him our thanks, for he uses our hands to do the work.'

Goha nodded.

'You remember the chief who visited us yesterday?'

'*Eheh*, Bwana!'

'He told me he had an enemy in his jaw. *Kumbe*! When I looked into his mouth there was no doubt about it. The tooth was of small worth. It was as hollow as a buyu tree.'

Goha smiled. 'I heard the words, Bwana, how he had praise for the medicine that stops pain. I saw how you struggled with his tooth. *Kumbe*, it was with difficulty that I did not laugh when you said, Bwana, that you would sooner have a dead hyaena under your bed than a dead tooth in your head.'

'*Hongo*! It was easier to listen than to do the work, but, believe me, I had large satisfaction when I saw that tooth with its twisted roots in a dish.'

Seko suddenly pricked his ears. We looked towards the hospital gate.

'*Kumbe*! Goha, here comes the one who probably had the greatest satisfaction in our work.'

I walked towards the cavalcade, who were crowding into the courtyard talking excitedly in Swahili. I greeted them in that language.

'*Jambo*, Bwana *Mkubwa*!'

'*Jambo*, Bwana.'

'*Habari*? What is the news?'

'*Habari njema*, the news is good.'

The Chief stood in front of me with his mouth wide open, pointing to the place where his tooth had been.

'Bwana, it is gone. With it has gone my pain. Last night I lay down and slept, and although there is the feeling in my mouth of raw meat, *yoh*, I have joy in your work. And behold, I have brought you a gift.'

Dramatically he signalled and through the gate was led a woebegone donkey. He took the rope in his hand and then came across and placed it in mine.

'This, Bwana, is my thank you for the removal of my tooth.'

I could feel Daudi beside me shaking with laughter. Goha was looking at my gift carefully. It in turn was looking carefully at his small dog, who kept well out of range of what looked like experienced feet. 'Thank you,' I returned. 'It is a gift of great originality.'

'Bwana,' said the Chief, 'I would have joy to receive a gift from you of some of those pills that stopped pain.'

I gave them to him, and we watched him move off down the hill with his followers.

'*Yoh*,' grinned Daudi, 'Bwana, this is a donkey that is a grandfather many times over. His bones are full of age. Feed him, however, and before long strength will return to his legs.'

The donkey lifted his head and looked at him in a way that made me feel he understood every word that was spoken.

'*Yoh*.' Goha put his arm round the creature's neck. 'He is a donkey of character.'

'*Koh*,' grunted Daudi, 'he is only a donkey of small worth.'

I laughed. 'No. There is real value in this donkey.

34

Tie him up, Goha. Behold, I will give you the task of looking after him. Seko can help you.'

For a long minute dog looked at donkey and donkey looked at dog. The little creature's tail started to wag and his large companion opened his mouth wide and brayed loud and long.

Goha smiled. 'I shall call him Punda.'

He led him away and tied him to a thorn tree. 'Yes, Seko, dogs are good animals and fine companions but God has used donkeys to do his work again and again. You and I must have respect for Punda.'

In a week the bedraggled donkey had changed considerably. Goha was grooming him with a piece of old blanket.

'He is becoming an animal of importance, is Punda.'

The boy looked up, automatically covering his right eye. 'He has joy, Bwana. I feed him with care because his stomach is elderly and I rub his hide with strength till it shines.'

'How is the second dog I ever operated on?'

Seko wagged his tail and undoubtedly grinned. Goha smiled delightedly. 'Truly, Bwana, this donkey of ours, like Seko, has the ability to laugh with his eyes.'

As he spoke, the donkey threw back his head and brayed. Seko barked excitedly. 'They're friends, Bwana. They talk much together.'

'Punda is not only for ornament. I want you to take him to the villages and bring to the hospital some of those who need our medicine. Punda will carry them slowly. You will lead him. Behold, each day you become stronger. Soon I shall do your operation.'

Goha's face glowed with excitement. 'Bwana, first remove the *ipu* - the swelling, that is in my back.' He slipped off the cloth that covered his body, displaying an ugly lump as big as two closed fists. 'It irritates. It is in the way. I can't rest properly while it is there, Bwana.'

'Sin is exactly like that, Goha. It twists, it irritates, it grows and disturbs your rest. It's a cruel, cramping, crippling thing and, strangely enough, people don't bother about it. They shrug and try to pretend it isn't there.'

'Bwana, I don't shrug and deceive myself about my back and chest and my face that is twisted and gives me shame.'

'Perhaps your trouble is really a blessing because it helps you to understand and fear this soul-crippling trouble.'

Goha opened his mouth but no word came, for Punda filled the air again with donkey music as Daudi came up.

'Ready to operate, doctor?'

'Coming, Daudi. Goodbye, Goha. Ask God to lead you along the right path. You need a rope to guide donkeys, but a prayer is the way with God's children.'

We went into the operating room together. Through the windows I watched a boy, a dog and a donkey walking purposefully in the direction of a village beyond the grove of baobab trees called Kibuyu.

An hour later Goha, the donkey, and the dog arrived at Kibuyu. They stood at a distance from a group who gaped at a large man who squatted in the shade, groaning.

'Great pain!' he moaned. '*Hongo*, it is as though fire burns in my big toes. It flares and dies down, and flares and dies down. Surely *machisi* - devils, blow upon the flames. *Hooeei*!'

'*Kah*,' muttered a scared voice, 'surely this is a matter of spells.'

'*Eheh*,' came a muted chorus of agreement.

Goha peered through the legs of those that stood in front of him. He stroked his small dog's ears and whispered, 'The Bwana said to watch and see and to remember.' Seko looked at him with understanding eyes. At the far end of the village, a lame man was shaping a stool from a log of wood. Goha walked through the shadows to join him.

'Bwana Chigoda, you and I know they can help him at the hospital. Should I offer to give him a ride there on Punda's back?'

The stool carver paused. 'Do it, Goha, but not yet. Woga can behave with cunning.'

At dusk Goha came to my door. '*Hodi*, Bwana?'

'*Karibu*, Goha. What's happened?'

'Bwana, I've found a sick one. He has sickness in his feet, especially in his big toes, and there is hot anger in his heart.'

'*Hongo*! What's his name?'

'He is Woga, the mushroom.'

'*Kumbe*, I remember him. Is he not a well-known singer in the Ugogo country?'

'Bwana, he only sings in the way people praise

when he drinks *pombe* - beer. *Heeh*, he can drink half a debiful in an hour.'

I calculated quickly: half a kerosene tin full – twenty litres – in an hour! He must be one with considerable capacity.

Goha went on. 'And eat! It is said he can eat as much as any two others, but *ooh*, these days he has no joy. He has *wuvimbo*, a swelling, Bwana, on each of his feet where his big toe meets his foot. It swells and it shines and it gives him no joy. The witchdoctor has treated him. He says it is the work of devils and has given him charms to wear round his neck, but they give him no help.'

I drew a rough diagram on a piece of paper and gave him a red pencil. 'Mark on this where these swellings are and what they look like.'

For a while Goha was busy and then handed the paper back to me.

'Behold, Bwana, his knees, his wrists, his elbows, his ankles, his thumbs and his big toes.'

'Was he stiff?'

'*Eheh*, Bwana. He tried to stand on his feet but could not.'

'*Hongo*!' I pulled open a drawer and took out a bottle. 'This is the medicine which is the complete answer to his trouble, which we call gout. But the pills will do no good if they remain in the bottle. They must be swallowed after he has eaten – two after dawn, two when the sun is overhead, two at sunset. But he is *mukamu* - a violent person, Goha. Let us ask for the powerful help of God in the matter.'

We did so, kneeling beside the dispensing bench. When we stood up some minutes later my young companion asked, 'Did God hear, Bwana?'

'He always hears.'

'Will he answer?'

'Yes, he always answers in the way he sees best. He loves to help, especially when it's something like this that we're trying to do for him.'

Goha nodded. 'I wonder what he will do?'

'We'll know that later on. *Hongo!* You'll have a story to tell me. There is always adventure in working for God. But suppose you wait till tomorrow. Tonight Woga will be expecting the medicines of the witchdoctor to relieve him. But tomorrow, after a night of pain, he will be more ready to take our medicines.'

Goha agreed. He then put Seko carefully into the padded box which was under his bed.

4
Twisted Mushroom

Daudi took me aside gently. 'Doctor, do you still plan to operate on Goha?'

'Yes, Daudi, there may be three separate operations. First I'll remove the coconut-sized lump from the small of his back. After that we'll see how he stands up to things before we tackle the swelling on his shoulder blade and the twisting of his face.'

From under the pepper trees came the tinkle of a skilfully played *ilimba*. We looked across and saw a stocky figure wearing a long white *kanzu* and a red *fez* perched on the side of his head. He was making music much to the liking of three small boys and an old man who leaned on a spear.

I pointed with my chin to the broad-shouldered man.

'Who is that, Daudi?'

'He comes from near the equator, doctor, way out west of here on the shores of Lake Victoria.'

We stood listening and as he finished we went forward.

'*Jambo*,' I greeted, speaking in Swahili.

'*Jambo*, Bwana.'

'How are you?'

'Well, but…' He went into a long string of details. I listened carefully and then asked, 'What is your name?'

Daudi grinned and interrupted. 'His name is Chuma, which in English means Iron. *Yoh*, was he not so called because his voice is like the sound of beating on kerosene tins?'

Chuma moved as lithely as a leopard and in a twinkling he grabbed Daudi and held him struggling above his head while he asked with laughter in his voice, 'Bwana, have you some suitable thornbush into which I can throw this bundle of rubbish?'

Nusu and Mboga came running over. I laughed as Daudi, struggling vainly, said, 'I was mistaken, doctor. He has a rich, deep voice like the sound of a large drum, oh, most mellow and good.'

Chuma chuckled. 'He learns fast, this one, Bwana. It will not be long before he will also sing the songs of the people of the Lake district.'

Daudi was replaced on his feet. He rolled his eyes.

'*Yoh*! You have disturbed my inside. It is upside-down and grumbles.'

Mboga broke in. 'His name is Chuma, Bwana, for he is a *fundi* - an expert, when it comes to making things out of iron.'

'Is that so, Chuma?'

'*Eheh*! Bwana, see my hands.' They were the hands of a blacksmith alright.

He came with me and I listened to all the details of his sickness. Daudi did routine tests.

'Tomorrow we shall know exactly how best to help you,' I told him.

Early the next morning I watched Goha and Seko and Punda, the elderly donkey, proceeding down the hill towards the village where the man with gout lived.

They moved sedately along the path to Woga's house. In the shade lay the sick man, his head in his hands. As Goha watched, a spasm seemed to run through his bulky frame. He screwed up his face with pain. Goha asked quietly, '*Mzee*, Oh Elder of the Tribe, there is no joy in your feet?'

Woga spat. '*Kah*!' There was a wealth of agreement, disgust and despair in that one word.

Goha went on. 'There are strong medicines for troubles such as yours in the hospital.'

'What do you know of things like this?' shouted Woga angrily. 'Are you a *muganga* - a medicine man?'

Goha shook his head. 'No, for their work is one of small profit. Have you not swallowed medicines and been rubbed with the rubbing fat?'

Woga groaned and mumbled and then demanded gruffly, 'Tell me of your medicines. What roots do you cook? What portions of a goat do you mix with the powdered teeth of a leopard?'

Goha shook his head and pointed with his chin at Seko.

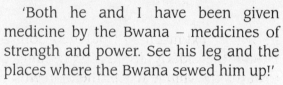

'Both he and I have been given medicine by the Bwana – medicines of strength and power. See his leg and the places where the Bwana sewed him up!'

'Has the Bwana medicines to overcome the pain that burns and throbs?'

'*Eheh*, that exactly.'

'*Hongo*, it is a long safari to that place with feet like mine, Small One.'

'For this very reason I have brought Punda. He is an animal of understanding.'

Some considerable time later a sick man and a tired donkey reached the hospital.

Goha ran inside excitedly. 'Bwana, he's here. Punda and I have done our part of the work. You have only to cure him now.'

Before long Woga lay in bed, a bed that sagged under his weight, for he was of ample size. He frowned heavily. '*Yoh*, Bwana, my feet have pain bulging through them.'

'You suffered somewhat on the safari on the back of that donkey?'

Woga rolled his eyes expressively.

'We can help much with injections and in other ways, but there are things to know about this disease. Let me first remove the pain and have you walking about again, then we will talk many words as to the cause and the way to stop further attacks.'

Behind me stood Chuma, the blacksmith. 'Bwana, have you medicine for me also?'

'*Ngheeh*! You have a disease called Bilharzia. Daudi will give you injections every day.'

The blacksmith's mouth fell open. 'He will do it? He who I held over my head? *Ah*! Why did I not know this before?'

Daudi looked solemn. 'It is a medicine of strength, this. Inject it into the wrong place and there is discomfort, often ulcers, sometimes abscesses, always pain and throbbing and…'

Mboga slapped Chuma on the shoulder and burst out laughing. '*Yoh*, hammer swinger, your future is full of possibilities!'

Chuma looked from one to the other of us and then his face wrinkled in a smile. '*Hongo*, this is a place of laughter. I will have joy to stay here.'

46

'I'll give you your first injection now, Chuma.' He followed me round to the dispensary. Outside the door sat Seko, ears up, tail busily wagging.

The broad man laughed. '*Jambo*, smiling dog. How is your appetite?'

Seko grinned at him and limped over, looking into his face.

'So you like dogs, Chuma?'

'*Eheh*, Bwana. Animals of friendship.'

'This one's owner is a sick boy. He will have joy in your singing and musical instruments.'

I filled the syringe and blew out the bubbles. Chuma braced his legs and set his jaw. Obviously he feared the worst. The corner of his mouth twitched as the needle went in. He held his mouth and shut his eyes tight. A few seconds later I rolled down his sleeve.

'*Yoh*! It's a prickle and nothing more. I thought...'

He laughed as I nodded. 'Your fear was to no purpose.'

Goha stood behind me. 'Bwana, when will you take away my lumps?'

'Before long.'

'Tomorrow, Bwana? Please do it soon!' Tears filled his eyes.

'Now, this very minute we will test the strength of your blood.'

In the afternoon Mboga handed me a slip of paper: Goha, Haemoglobin 62 per cent. I paused. There was risk but I decided to take it. 'We'll do it tomorrow early.'

'Thank you, Bwana doctor.'

Chuma seemed to sense the tension. From the bag over his shoulder he produced an *ilimba* decorated with beads, leopard skin and minute mirrors. His thumbs worked fast, producing a tune that made my mind swing back to my grandmother's music box.

Goha squatted and listened. Suddenly Seko put his head back and howled.

A surly voice came from inside the ward. 'Even a dog has small joy in that row.'

Chuma stopped and asked softly, 'Who was that?'

Goha whispered, 'Woga, the man with pain in his feet who once was a *fundi* singer and dancer. He is also a man of strength and bad temper.'

The blacksmith spat and leaned over a box of bits of iron, bolts and odd washers and nuts. He picked out a length of iron bar thicker than a poker and somewhat longer and bent it into a U-shape with his powerful hands.

'Man of strength! Do that then! Swollen hands lack strength.'

Daudi appeared on the scene. He could feel trouble in the air. He produced an old spiral spring from the box of bits and pieces. '*Hongo*, many can bend things. It is a matter of strength only. Baboons can bend and tear and break but it takes skill of a special kind to make crooked things straight.'

Chuma felt the spring. '*Yoh*,' he grinned, 'it could be done, but it would be indeed a work of skill. I would like to do it, for this is the sort of iron that is best for making *ilimbas*.'

Goha had been bending over the box. He held up a length of narrow glass tubing. 'Can you straighten the spring, oh *fundi*, so that it passes through the tube without stopping?'

Chuma laughed. 'I will do it, Small One. You shall help me when you rest after the Bwana's work on your lumps.'

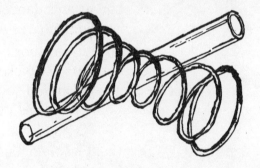

5
Dangerously Close

Woga stood at the hospital gate, using the strong post to support himself.

'Bwana, my feet are still sore.'

'What of your elbows and thumbs and knees?'

'Better a little.'

'Today I'm going to do a work of difficulty on the child who helped you.'

Woga shrugged. '*Yoh*! My legs ache.'

I walked on. Under the pepper trees sat Chuma, his silent *ilimba* beside him.

'*Jambo*, Bwana.'

'*Jambo*.'

'You will cut the boy with your small knife?'

'*Eheh*.'

'Cut with skill, Bwana. He is a child of courage. Work with hands that bring swift healing.'

Goha lay on the operating table while I prepared to give him the anaesthetic.

'Bwana,' he whispered, 'I've been waiting for this moment for days. I've thought about it and feared it, and longed for it to come and now it is here.'

'It always happens that way and the time always comes – the time for things we look forward to and the time for things we don't. Sometimes we wait longer than others but it always comes. But now, let us talk to the One we cannot see but who is always here. His own words are, "I will never leave you nor forsake you." Comforting?'

'Good words, Bwana, especially when your heart beats as mine does now.'

We prayed together and then the boy drifted into a deep sleep. Gently we rolled him on his side and the operation started.

A dog's long dismal howling came from outside as I took up the instruments.

'*Yoh*,' said Daudi through his hospital mask, 'that dog has small joy in the work that we do on his master.'

'*Eheh*, Daudi, and I share his feelings. This is no ordinary lump. There is something unusual about it.'

Working cautiously I snipped fibre by fibre until the ugly lump was in full view. Its roots went uncomfortably close to the spinal cord.

I turned to the nurse working with us. 'Wendwa, count his pulse, please.'

She bent down and held his wrist. 'Pulse regular, Bwana, 110 beats to the minute.'

'Keep your finger on it and prepare the shock tray. I don't like the way things are going. We may have problems.

'Daudi, the forceps and the catgut. I'm going to sew him up in a moment. And stop the anaesthetic altogether. This is the critical stage.' Quickly the scissors snipped. The tumour was away and gone.

With a sigh of relief I started to stitch up. The last dressing was in place when Perisi breathed, 'Bwana, his pulse! It's stopped.'

I wrenched off a glove and slipped my hand over his heart but there was no sign of beating. Outside, the small dog started to howl mournfully.

'*Yoh*,' shivered Wendwa, 'little Seko thinks his master is dead.'

'He knows that the boy's life is in danger. Now quickly, that shock tray.'

I filled a syringe and injected and then rhythmically began pressing on his chest.

'Perisi, feel any pulse?'

'Not yet, Bwana, but there seems to be a twitching.'

'Put the stethoscope into my ears and hold the chest piece over his heart. There, that's it.'

For a few moments I concentrated on listening. There was a faint sound.

The small dog howled miserably outside.

I grabbed a tube, slipped it into the boy's mouth and into his lung. We had no oxygen supply in that jungle hospital. I made the best of what we had and breathed down that tube. Nothing seemed to happen, then through the stethoscope came the faint but definite sound of the heart beating. I listened, holding my breath, and then Goha sighed a small sigh.

'Thank God, he's alive, Bwana!' Wendwa was excited.

'He's alive, yes, but we must work on.'

'Feel his pulse now,' burst out Daudi. 'Thank you, Lord Jesus.'

'Yes, Lord,' murmured Wendwa.

I echoed my thanks with deep feeling.

Seko stopped howling and curled up in the shade.

'*Yoh*, that small dog has an understanding that goes deep,' said Wendwa.

Goha's pulse became stronger and he breathed by himself. Daudi and I wiped our foreheads and both exclaimed, '*Wooh*!'

'*Kah*, doctor, did I pray!'

'*Hongo*, didn't we all? Thank God he's all right now.'

'He's been undernourished for a long time and his heart muscle is weak. He has also had malaria and all sorts of other tropical troubles.'

'But why did you put that tube down his throat?'

'It was the only way we had to get carbon dioxide, that gas that sends "let me breathe more" messages to the brain. Remember in the Old Testament how the prophet Elisha breathed into the body of the small boy who had died?'

They nodded.

'Well, that is the same thing occurring thousands of years ago – the first time that artificial respiration was ever mentioned in any book as far as I know.'

I sat beside the boy for an hour. He at last came out of the anaesthetic and said sleepily, 'Bwana, has it gone?'

'Yes, Goha, it's gone.'

'Good. *Asante*, Bwana, thank you.' He yawned and slept.

Outside the door the small dog limped over, making efforts to talk and wagging his tail fast and hard. I bent down and patted his head.

'It was a near thing, Seko. You and I would have had much sorrow if we hadn't started his heart again, *heh*?'

The dog grinned at me, squatted down outside the door and put his head on his paws.

Woga limped out of the shadows. Daudi spoke softly, 'Doctor, Woga boils with anger. He scorns the small white pills and he has strong desire for the coloured capsules.'

'He is a trouble maker. Watch him carefully, Daudi.'

Woga went to the ward where Mboga was working. Speaking behind his hand he urged, 'I will give you a goat for a handful of those medicines the size of a peanut that are half green and half red.'

Mboga shook his head. 'They are not for your sickness and will do you no good. Anyhow, I don't sell hospital medicines, it's stealing.'

'A goat,' urged Woga, 'a fine goat – this is a way of much profit.'

'But useless. If you had the stabbing disease that would be different, but your trouble will have no benefit.'

The man with the swollen feet snorted with rage and rasped through clenched teeth, 'I shall have what I want. No one shall stop me!'

Seko was outside the ward door next morning when I came to see my young patient.

'*Mbukwa*, Bwana.'

'*Mbukwa*, Goha. What of your back?'

'Bwana, I can lie on it. *Kah*, there is strong satisfaction in doing a new thing.'

'Truly. You have no pain, no soreness?'

'No, Bwana. But was there trouble?'

'*Eheh*, there was indeed. Your body has small strength and there will be much swallowing of medicines before more work can be done by my little knife.'

Goha nodded slowly. 'I shall take the medicine, Bwana.'

'Do that, and in the meantime lie quietly and sleep.'

Three days passed. On the evening of the third day Nusu had people singing in the moonlight. Goha lay in bed and I sat beside him. The small dog's ears were silhouetted against the whitewash of the dispensary wall.

The boy noticed this and smiled. 'Seko keeps on recovering, Bwana.'

'*Eheh*! He is a splendid patient.'

He nodded. 'He brings me deep joy.' He lay quietly for a while and then looked up. 'What is happening tonight?'

'After the singing they will hear the story of Noah and his sons and his huge boat.'

We looked through the door. A hurricane lantern was all that lit the sixty or so people who crowded around the portable gramophone. Daudi wound it up and from its revolving disc came the story of the ark and the great flood and of how nearly everyone had turned their backs on God.

As the last words came from the record, a voice was heard further down the ward. 'Why shouldn't people rejoice? Why shouldn't they have their fun in their own way?'

'You can do what you like, Big Toe,' came another voice. 'God won't stop you, but he tells us quite clearly we'll pay for what we take.'

'*Kah*!' came Woga's voice. 'I don't mind paying.'

Chuma from the far end of the ward said bluntly, 'That's a different tale from the one you told us on the day when your toe throbbed and you filled the countryside with your groaning.'

Woga sat bolt upright. '*Yoh*, for a stranger you are full of words. It would give me joy to pull you apart like the hyaena did the boy's dog.'

A cry came from Goha's lips. I stood up. '*Basi* – enough! Lie down, Woga.'

Reluctantly he did so, grumbling deeply under his breath.

I walked over to Chuma. 'No brawling, blacksmith.'

He grinned and said softly, '*Yoh*, he makes me boil inside, that one. Truly he has turned his back to God.'

'What about you, then?'

He drew his knees up and peered at me as he clasped them with his muscular arms. 'Bwana, I should have liked to have helped Noah with that ark.'

'Are you sure? Would you not have made jokes at the builders and scorned their warnings?'

'A few days ago, yes, Bwana, but not now.'

'Well, where are you? In the ark in safety or still outside in danger?'

Chuma shook his head slowly. 'There is much food for thinking. It takes time to digest.'

'Think carefully. We will talk again of the matter.'

Woga was glowering in my direction. I went back to him, but first spoke to Goha.

'Have you pain in the place where the stitches are?'

The boy nodded and whispered, 'It gets worse at night. Seko feels it too where you sewed him up. Does he not make the small noises of pain?'

I gave him two pain controlling pills. He swallowed them and sank back on his pillow.

A large hand touched my shoulder. Woga spoke softly. 'Bwana, do not have anger towards me.'

I smiled. 'We are at peace, you and I. But don't fight with people. What worries your mind?'

'There are those that say that a spell has been cast against me and it is a thing of fear.'

'This is not witchcraft. It is a trouble that I know well. It is common in many countries, but uncommon here. The disease is called gout and is built into you, Woga.'

'*Kah*! Built into me? How, Bwana? What do you mean?'

'It is a thing of common knowledge that some have legs of unequal length, others have eyes that are not straight, some are born with six fingers on each hand and some have gout.

'Often the trouble lies quietly within you like a scorpion under a stone. Then one day something unusual happens – a feast, perhaps, of beer and the inside meats of an animal like liver and kidney. These things set this disease on fire.'

Woga's lip twisted. His voice was loaded with sarcasm. 'They have been telling you about me, Bwana. This is your cunning way to stop me eating and drinking the things I like! What I need is the strong medicine you would use if you had my trouble.'

He grunted, spat, and turned his back on me.

6

Corkscrew Dudu

'Bwana,' the voice was urgent. 'Come to the place of sick ones quickly!'

I was wide awake in a second when I recognised Wendwa's voice.

'What is the matter?'

'Bwana, Goha is sick – temperature 40°, pulse 120, respiration rate 24.'

We hurried to the hospital.

The boy lay propped up in bed looking drawn and anxious. His teeth chattered so noisily that the oddest sounds came through the stethoscope. One thing was obvious – his heart was beating at a tremendous rate. I listened to his chest. There was normal breathing – no pneumonia.

'Daudi, will you take some of his blood and look at it under the microscope? This is a matter of urgency.'

As he did so, I examined the operation wound. All sorts of alarming possibilities went through my mind.

There was no way of telling what would be found when the dressings came off. I feared the worst but the whole thing was completely normal. He must have developed one of the tropical fevers which attack so frequently in Africa.

I put my hand on Goha's shoulder and said, 'This is fever. We have the medicine for it. Lie quietly, relax and try to sleep.'

I went over to the pathology room. Seko sat outside the door, his head tilted questioningly. Bending down to pat him I said, 'He'll be all right, Seko, or at least I hope so.'

The dog looked at me with large eyes full of understanding. There was no question mark in them now.

Daudi was staining the glass slide.

'What do you think it is, doctor?'

'It could be anything, ordinary or extraordinary – any one of the tropical fevers, the early stages of pneumonia or a really bad complication of this operation. It's too early to know exactly what we're facing unless that microscope of yours can help. Whatever it is we must work quickly. He's dangerously sick at the moment.'

I went to the dispensary and took some aspirin tablets from a bottle. Outside the door stood Woga. We walked together towards the ward.

'Bwana, is his sickness great?'

'His actual sickness is probably no worse than yours, but he has no strength to fight it, while you…' I poked his flabby muscles.

He nodded.

'We'll know his trouble soon and then we can treat it. Microscopes and other instruments help us to find exactly what the sickness is and then we can give him the special medicine for it. There's no guessing, no wild hoping about this hospital.'

I went across to Goha's bed, supporting him as he swallowed the pills. 'These will help you for the moment, Goha. They will cool you down and stop the pain and shivering.'

'*Asante*, Bwana, thank you.' He lay still for a while, murmuring as the medicine started to work, 'Truly, Bwana, I have much sickness.'

'*Eheh*, Goha, but we have medicine for you. Lie quietly, rest and, if you can, sleep.'

He lay with his eyes wide open until Daudi came in.

'Doctor, I have the report.' He handed me a slip of paper on which was written, 'Spirillum + + +.'

'*Hongo*, heavy infection, eh Daudi?'

He nodded. 'Tick Fever. Bwana, his blood is swarming with the tiny *dudus*. It looks as though there are a thousand tiny corkscrews all tangled round each other mixed with his blood cells.'

Goha caught these words. '*Yoh*, Bwana, it is a hard matter for me to escape from twisted things.'

'You're right there, but fortunately we have a strong medicine that helps us to untwist this fever. We call it tick fever. Let's deal with your sickness first, and then before long you'll be able to help others.'

'Is the medicine pills?'

'No, its *sindano* - the needle.'

'*Yoh*, Bwana.' He put his face into the pillow and his shoulders shook.

I sat at the ward table and wrote for a while. Daudi came in with a tray. Goha heard him and stretched out his arm silently. I gave the injection to the tense boy whose teeth chattered with fear but whose arm was as firm as a rock. I rubbed the spot gently where the needle had been.

He smiled up at me. '*Yoh*, Bwana, I'm glad that's over.'

The sound of drumming and singing was coming softly through my window. It was Woga with a group of admirers around him.

I stood in the doorway. 'That was food for the ears, oh music *fundi*. Does your toe behave?'

Woga squatted over his drum and shook his head. 'I am half better, Bwana. The swelling is smaller, the pain is less but what remains gives me no joy.'

'Swallow medicine with strength and when the moon is new the mail from England arrives and I will be able to give special help.'

On the far side of the ward under the pepper trees sat Chuma looking glum.

'*Habari*, blacksmith,' I greeted. 'What news?'

He replied, using the routine African reply, '*Mzuri*, Bwana, good – but bad.'

'Then where is the worm in the corncob, Chuma?'

'*Yoh*, Bwana, that Woga. *Kah*!' He spat. 'He irritates me, he…' he leapt to his feet. '*Yoh*, Bwana, I…' Chuma grunted. 'My head aches. Within me the white ants of pain gnaw.'

'*Kumbe*! Is that so? How did your injection go today?'

'Bwana, he's a *fundi*, that Daudi. He hurt me less than you did.' He laughed.

'Let me tell you about your disease. Is it your habit to swim in the waters of Lake Tanganyika?'

'*Eheh*, Bwana, I have joy to do this.'

I held up a glass bottle. Inside were some small water-snail shells.

'Do these creatures live in the water on the weeds near where you swim?'

'*Eheh*, Bwana, many of those.'

'*Hongo*. In that water is a tiny *dudu* that is shaped like this…' the peanut gardens were in front of me. They had just been watered. I took up a small lump of clay, shaped it into the size and shape of an almond nut and then stuck a thorn through it so that the point protruded sharply.

'It is a tiny *dudu* that looks like this. They hook into your skin, make their way into your system and lay their eggs. Through your blood they go until they come into the part of you near the liver and then, behold, the egg hatches and out comes an ugly, twisted worm.'

Chuma rolled his eyes. '*Hongo*! A worm, you say. I've always felt some sort of *dudu* crawled within me.'

'The *dudu* that lays the eggs is only a small thing, but strong. It can lived for years – ten, twenty or even more.'

'*Kah*, this is a thing of small happiness! What does it do there, gnaw holes like the white ant?'

'No, but it is most diligent in laying its eggs and they produce all the trouble. Now, if the problem was an ordinary snake who produced many eggs and hid them in your garden, what would you do?'

Chuma chuckled. 'Kill the snake, dig up the eggs and squash them.'

'Right. This is the method we use also. The medicine that you are given daily is one of no joy for worms and also it destroys the shell of the eggs.'

'*Yoh*! A medicine of thoroughness, truly.'

'As you say, but it takes time.'

A nurse came up. 'Bwana, Goha has a temperature that is normal. He also has desire to eat.'

'Good, he may do so. The more he eats, the better I like it. Come, Chuma, we'll visit him.'

Goha looked like a limp rag. Seko peered through the door, his eyes fixed on his master, and whined. 'He would have joy to be closer to me, Bwana.' Goha caught Wendwa's eye and hurried on to say, 'But I understand he must stay out there.'

I nodded and felt his pulse. 'Things are better now, but it's bed for you for days yet.'

'Could I lie in the sun, Bwana?'

Chuma spoke eagerly. 'I will carry him, bed and all, to the place where I plan to work tomorrow.' He picked up the spring Goha had given him. 'He wants me to make this absolutely straight, Bwana!'

'*Eheh*, it is a good thing.'

'A work of difficulty, though. Is it not coiled and crooked and complicated? What do you want this done for, Goha?'

'The Bwana and I like untwisting things.' The boy paused.

'And people,' I added.

'And people, Bwana?'

'Yes, disease and sickness twist the body and give pain.'

'*Eheh*! Pain certainly twists. But why straighten the spring?' insisted Chuma.

'When you work with your hammer, talk with Goha. The matter will then become clear.'

7

Straight and Narrow

Chuma had collected the tools he needed to start work. A length of railway track was the anvil. He made a forge of some pottery and a goatskin which he had sewn to make foot-bellows. Charcoal was glowing as he blew briskly, the coiled spring in front of him.

Goha was sitting up in bed in the shade looking better, though still rather wobbly. He spoke.

'Did you see in the Bwana's microscope the shape of the *dudu* that caused your trouble?'

Chuma nodded.

'Did you see the one that caused mine?'

Chuma nodded again. 'It was a small thing that looked rather like this spring, all coiled and twisted.'

'Truly,' agreed Goha. 'The Bwana says that a tick bit me and that these *dudus* came from its mouth and that they bred inside me.'

'*Eheh*, and the Bwana has explained to me about my disease also. *Yoh*, this hospital is a place of wisdom.'

Beside the blacksmith's tools was the goatskin bag in which he kept his *ilimba*.

'May I look at your *ilimba*?'

Chuma nodded as he heated the spring until it glowed red. The boy's thumb moved tentatively over the box-like musical instrument with its various lengths of flat steel. Then he produced a tune.

The blacksmith was beating with his hammer on the anvil as the hot spring was gradually straightened out.

'*Yoh*, Small One! You have some skill in playing that.'

'*Hongo*,' Goha glowed, 'but I have small chance to make music because I have no *ilimba* of my own.'

Chuma spat on the red-hot iron, hammered it and twanged it with his thumb. 'This is the sort of stuff that might be useful to make an *ilimba*. Behold, perhaps the Bwana has wood and we could make one for you.'

'*Yoh*, that would be wonderful. *Kumbe*, you're straightening out that spring all right.' He looked at Chuma fairly between the eyes. 'Are you twisted inside?'

The muscular African placed his hand tenderly over his stomach. '*Eheh*, *yoh*, there are pains within me. But the Bwana's medicine will cure them.'

'But I am not talking about your body. I am talking about your *mitima*, the part of you that the Bwana has no medicine for or, at any rate, no medicine that he can inject through needles. It is not the work of *dudus* to twist your soul, it is the evil cunning of Shaitan, the Devil himself.'

'*Hongo*, how do you know these words?'

'The Bwana and Daudi have told me. They read to me from God's book. It is a book of special importance.'

'*Yoh*, how do you know when your soul's twisted?'

'When your body is twisted you have pain. When your soul is twisted you have fear. There is that small voice inside you that warns you and tells you.'

'*Kumbe*!' Chuma put his hammer down. 'And if the voice no longer speaks?'

Goha pointed with his chin to the children's ward. 'In there is a boy who was charged by a buffalo. He is paralysed. He has no strength, no feeling in his legs. He calls himself Moja-Moja because one half of him works and the other half doesn't. Is it that your small voice that warns is like the part of him that does not work?'

'*Uh-huh*,' agreed the blacksmith, 'for the small voice is like my hands here.' He touched his palm with red-hot metal. '*Yoh*! It sizzles and smells.' He wrinkled up his nose. 'But it gives no pain.'

Goha's head nodded vigorously, 'Truly it burns your hand – you can see it, but you do not draw back.'

Chuma shrugged. 'My skin is so hard and tough that I feel little. It is the same with the small voice. I do not take much notice of it.'

'Have you no fear then?'

Chuma put down his tools and sat on the end of the bed. 'These days, Small One, I do have fear. Pain makes me remember.'

'*Eheh*,' agreed Goha. 'I have come close to death, *Hongo*, and I am glad that He made me straight.'

'He?'

'Yes, Jesus the Son of God. He came to make the crooked places straight. He came to straighten out where sin has twisted.'

'*Eeeh*,' said Chuma, 'maybe then my soul is twisted, but I can straighten it out. If I say I'll do a thing I'll do it all right.'

Seko, the small dog, came over and looked up at them both. Goha put out his hand for the spring.

'Great One, lend it to me for a moment.'

There was a hint of a smile round his face. He held the spring to his ear. An impish twist came to the corner of his mouth.

'Behold, I listen to the voice of the spring. Its voice is small and it says, "I have strength. I shall become straight all by myself if I have a mind to do so."'

Chuma picked up his hammer and looked at it with fine contempt. '*Yoh*, the words of a spring! *Eheeh*, it will become straight only if it is made so by the hand of a *fundi*.'

'*Kumbe*,' came the boy's voice, 'and man's soul is straightened out only by the hand of God himself. God says so. God's book says you don't deserve to have it done for you. It's not by what you do yourself, not by what you achieve, but by putting yourself into his hands – hands that have scars in them.'

'Scars?'

'*Eheh*, they drove great nails through his hands. They nailed him to a tree and he died.'

'What for?'

'So that he could take the twists out of our lives.'

'I don't understand it,' said Chuma.

'You will.'

The blacksmith picked up the spring and attacked it hard.

When I came to the ward later that day he had finished.

'*Yoh*, blacksmith, you have done it.'

'*Eheh*, Bwana. I am going into the ward to show Goha my work.'

The boy lay in bed and was intrigued to see the long length of flattened-out iron pass without a hitch through the glass tube.

'*Hongo*, Chuma, the spring couldn't straighten itself out?'

He shook his head. 'Bwana, it isn't the nature of springs to do that.'

'Truly, neither can men straighten out the twists that sin puts into their lives. There must be outside help. And in the matter of the twisting of the soul, it is only God who can do that for us.'

8
Sweat of Brow

Goha was up and almost himself again. He came to me. 'Bwana, Woga has sorrow in his feet and knees and he says you promised to give him strong special medicine.'

'He shall have small white pills for five days and then the sweat treatment.'

'*Kah*! What is the sweat treatment?'

'Find a wide-necked bottle, place it under the tap and start the water dripping slowly.' He ran off.

Woga limped towards me. '*Eheh*, Bwana. My feet, *yoh*! My knees, *yoh*, *heeh*! and *kumbe*, my elbows and hands…'

Goha had returned and placed the bottle under the slow drip of the tap.

'Watch this,' I said, 'and understand your sickness clearly.'

Woga sat on a stool and fixed his eyes on the bottle. Half-an-hour later I returned to my door.

Woga spoke grumpily, 'The bottle now overflows. This is a thing that a child could see and know.'

'*Hongo*! Tell me, is the ground beneath the bottle now dry or wet?'

'*Kah*! Is it not wet?'

'Remember that. Let the matter settle well between your ears. This is a picture of what happens inside you when you have pains in your feet and toes.'

The large man wrinkled his forehead in amazement.

'In this sickness within you, your liver is in trouble. Its work is to remove the *taka taka*, the rubbish, the poisons that bring swelling and pain to your joints. Slowly their level rises as did the water in the bottle and then – *twa!* It overflows and suddenly your joints have burning pain.'

'You tell me words of truth?'

'I do.'

'Then why give me only small pills when my pain is large? Give me stronger medicine, the sort you would take yourself if your joints throbbed as mine do.' He stumbled to his feet and shook his fists at me.

'Take no notice of his anger,' murmured Mboga.

'Woga, to get rid of this poison we can help by sweating it out of you.'

Woga's voice shook with disgust. 'Sweat! *Kah*!'

'It is a matter of small trouble. You sit and let your skin work while you rest in the sun.'

'But how, Bwana?'

'Sit here on a stool. We will wrap you in blankets and rubber sheeting.'

Daudi went to a cupboard. 'Shall I bring waterproof sheeting and blankets?'

We draped the waterproof over Woga's large frame, tying the corners so that it would not fall off. Then the blanket was carefully wound round him and kept in place by a collar and a girdle of rope.

'Sing with energy,' I ordered. 'Others will join you and beat their drums.'

Woga did so, but after some time he stopped and his body sagged. '*Yoh*! I am weak. *Heeh*! I sweat. *Kumbe*! It runs out of me as never before. I am dry inside and dripping outside. How long must I cook this way?'

'Till *saa chenda*, the ninth hour, Woga, at least!'

'*Hongo*, I will be dried up altogether by then! This is a treatment of misery.'

'But pain is your enemy. Fight it with strength and joy. Here comes Nusu and others to sing. They will sit in the shade, however.'

'*Yoh*, it would be kindness to let me sit in the shade.'

'False kindness, for pain disappears with each gourd of sweat.'

Goha approached with a large gourd full of water. Woga tilted his head back and gulped down.

Carefully the boy tucked the blanket in at the neck and closely round the big man's feet. In a matter of minutes Woga started to sweat profusely again.

'*Yoh*,' he growled, 'this is like sitting in a cooking pot. *Weeeh*!'

Goha whispered, '*Yoh*! Bwana, Woga is in trouble. I fear that anger will soon grip him.'

Daudi tied a cloth round his forehead to stop sweat from trickling into his eyes. He must have lost litres of fluid through his sweat glands. His eyes looked heavy, his shoulders stooped and his head drooped. I unwrapped him and he staggered weakly to his feet and sat down suddenly.

'*Yoh*, am I not boiled? Has not all my strength run away?'

'Sit again, Bwana Woga,' Mboga encouraged. He stood on a box and with the hospital watering can poured a cool shower of water over the gouty one's bulky frame.

Woga turned and opened his mouth. Mboga obliged.

Then he stumbled into the shade, rolled over and fell asleep.

Chuma appeared. He was solemn. '*Kah*! I would have had joy to laugh at that baboon sweating as no man sweats, but it was better not.'

'I'm glad you didn't do that, blacksmith. Resentment is one of the really crooked things.'

'I'm beginning to understand that, for within me stirs a voice which cries warning.' He paused. 'Bwana, would it be possible for the boy and the dog and the donkey and myself to go walking in the villages?'

I nodded. 'First make a small trial safari in the neighbourhood of the hospital. Goha's strength is still small. If his feet drag, place him on the donkey.'

Away they went in single file.

Woga stretched, yawned hugely and sat up. He had slept solidly for three hours.

'Bwana, I feel wonderful. My feet feel new, my knees rejoice, my elbows, *heeh*! My thumbs and my toes, *yoh!*' He leapt in the air and gave a small gymnastic display then, puffing, he squatted down. 'Your medicines are full of wisdom.'

'So, Woga, you are better now as far as your body goes. You tried witchdoctor's medicine and found it didn't work. Then you sampled ours.'

Woga shrugged.

'In the matter of medicine for your body you chose our way. Now what about the disease of your soul?'

Woga drew designs in the dust with his toes. '*Kah*! You would rob me of my favourite pleasures.'

'And what of these things you regard as so important? What do they do for you?'

He growled. 'They bring discomfort to my body but…'

'Today you call it discomfort. Yesterday you called it agony. My work is to fight pain. Listen, Woga, remember we told you that if you choose to turn around and face God and ask him to forgive you and then set yourself to travel his paths, doing what he tells you then…'

Woga snorted irritably. 'But you wrench from me what I like best. You tie me down with words I am unwilling to follow.'

'But you give up pain, fear, insecurity, these unhappy things. You gain contentment, friendship and life after death.'

Woga lost his temper. He shouted, '*Hodu*! No more words of this sort. I return to my house to greet *lulu baha*, straight away.'

'Greet them then, but keep swallowing the little white pills three times a day and remember there are things you drink and eat that will bring your joints swelling, sadness and suffering.'

He limped away.

Daudi stood with me as we watched him staggering down the same path that Goha and his cavalcade had followed a few hours before.

Mboga came to my door.

'I have news of old Majimib. She has cooked a brew of beer and has taken it to Woga's house.'

9
Small Joy

The operation had taken two hours.

'*Kah*!' grunted Daudi as the last stitch went in. 'What a work that was, Bwana.'

I nodded. 'A little more than Ngoma, the witchdoctor, would have liked to tackle.'

Daudi wrinkled his nose. 'He makes people crooked, that one. His medicines are fear to fight fear. Ours are peace for pain.'

He looked up and pointed through the window. Coming through the gate was Chuma leading the donkey, with Goha perched on his shoulders.

'*Yoh*,' I laughed, 'which is the donkey?'

Punda chose that exact moment to advertise his arrival with an ear-splitting bray. A passenger sat hunched up dolefully on the animal's stern. But there was no sign of Seko.

On the steam-covered window Daudi traced two faces with his finger. 'See, Bwana, the mouth of Goha turns up at the end with a smile, while that of Small Joy who comes with him turns down.'

Goha stepped down from Chuma's shoulder and carefully helped his weary-looking charge to dismount and sit in the shade. He tied Punda to the umbrella tree and walked over to the operating theatre.

'*Kah*, Bwana, I have found a man filled with gloom.' He put on a quavering voice. '*Yoh*, the voice of donkeys brings misery to my poor head! *Kah*, the chatter of children is as the driving of nails into my eyes. If your stomach had within it snakes as vicious and active as mine you would *heeh*! know that misery is a way of small joy for such as I am.'

Goha's mimicry was notably accurate.

Daudi and I laughed. The boy went on. 'He is truly called Small Joy, Bwana. He holds his hands like this' (he draped his own hands sadly over his stomach) 'and misery fills his voice.' Goha's laughter stopped abruptly. 'Bwana, have you seen Seko here?'

'No, we thought he had followed you.'

The boy shook his head. 'I must go and find him.'

We went over to where the doleful man was squatting in the shade.

'*Mbukwa*,' I greeted.

'*Mbukwa*, Bwana. I have no joy in…'

I interrupted. '*Zo gono*? How did you sleep?'

'*Ale zo gono gwegwe.* How did you sleep?' he replied, and then went on, 'And how can I sleep when there is no joy in my stomach?'

'No joy whatsoever?'

'My tongue is dry as the sole of a sandal and is swollen and so…'

The miserable voice droned on, 'And Bwana,' he draped his hand over his stomach exactly as Goha had done, 'within me liver fights with spleen, and my thoughts by day and my thoughts by night are disturbed by the voices of several restless snakes.'

Even as he said this the oddest rumble came from within him and he produced explosive noises. Chuma looked solemn but his eyes were full of laughter. Small Joy rolled the muddy coloured whites of his eyes and groaned. 'Mine is a life of misery, misery, *eeh*!'

'In the matter of food, do you have joy?'

'*Kah*! Bwana, it is a matter of difficulty.'

'Suppose we give you milk to drink?'

'*Eheh*, Bwana, it pleases my mouth greatly but my throat refuses it.'

'*Hongo*, this is a thing of difficulty.'

'Eh, Bwana, difficulties, *yoh*! They surround me.'

'What about porridge?'

'*Koh*, Bwana, my mouth has small joy in it. It reaches my throat with peace, but my stomach refuses.'

'Come now, what happens when you have roasted meat?'

'*Eeh*, Bwana it is food for the nose and my stomach receives it with joy but it excites the snakes within me, and *ooh*, Bwana…' His hands caressed his thin abdomen and he belched. 'Hear them complain with strength.'

'We will work with strength. We will give you medicine for your interior but first you will be bathed and given the clothing of the hospital.'

'Bwana, is that necessary? Water on my skin always causes me sadness.'

'Yes, it is necessary, completely and utterly so!'

'*Hongo*, there is always sorrow coming my way.' Dejectedly he followed Daudi to the dispensary.

'Chuma, you and Goha have certainly brought in a man with a knot for a stomach.'

As if he sensed what was going on, Punda the donkey raised his lips to heaven and produced a bray of such strength that Chuma looked at me and grinned.

'Bwana, I felt all the way back that Punda wanted to laugh at the one who was on his back whose words were loaded with misery and wretchedness. I could feel Goha's mind working as he sat on my shoulders. Did he not shake with laughter at the words of that man of small happiness? And we whispered together collecting words of misery. When your heart sings inside you it is hard to be filled with gloom.'

'You're right there. You see our friend has not only trouble in his stomach but his soul is mouldy within him as well. We must definitely help him.'

But what a task it was! Small Joy, as everyone started calling him, had complaints, strong complaints, about

the medical tests that were given to him. But Daudi's jaw was fixed firmly and the full range were carried out.

I looked through all the results and recorded them.

'Bwana,' said Small Joy, 'I cannot swallow pills because of the thing in my throat. I cannot swallow powders because my stomach refuses them, and Bwana, the medicines that are in water, *eeeh*, I cannot take those because the restless snakes show strong disapproval.'

Daudi frowned. 'Be careful, the Bwana will give you medicine through a big needle that digs deep and produces strong burning pain in places where pain has never been before.'

'*Yoh*,' grieved Small Joy, 'perhaps Bwana I can swallow the medicine that is mixed with water, perhaps I can swallow the powders…'

'Perhaps you can,' grinned Daudi.

That evening Nusu started to sing folk stories of adventures with hyaenas. He accompanied the words with the up and down rhythm of a long bow-like instrument called a *singila*.

As I stopped to listen, Chuma came quietly to my side. 'Bwana, let us talk together.'

We walked up and down the moonlit path between the hospital buildings. My companion spoke with considerable emotion.

'Bwana, things have been happening to me. I have done many things in my life that I have tried to forget and almost succeeded. Since I have been here and heard the words of God and talked to young Goha and heard Daudi speak, Bwana, I feel that my soul is dirty. Bwana, I have asked Jesus, the Son of God, to forgive me and to make me clean.'

I gripped his hand. 'Chuma, this is the biggest happening in anyone's life. It is your second birthday. You have started to live. Your soul has come alive. But it's only the beginning. The first time you took an *ilimba* in your hand could you not make little music from it? But you practised and practised. God expects you to live his way and to obey him, then you find the full satisfaction of being a member of his family, of knowing you have eternal life.'

'*Hongo*, Bwana, this is a thing of wonder.' We parted quietly.

That night was full of drumming, wild rhythm and hectic singing. On my doorstep I saw a boy with his head in his hands.

In a muffled voice he said, 'Bwana, Seko has gone.'

Hurrying down the path swinging a lantern was Mboga. 'Seko is safe. He's in the medicine store room in your house.'

'Why did you hide him and how did you get him in?'

Mboga grinned. 'I did not trust Woga and Seko is small enough to fit through the window.'

I unlocked the door to see a white flash of dog – and Goha clasped his Seko delightedly.

10
Lion's Victim

Daudi dashed up to me. 'Doctor, an emergency! A herd boy has been injured by a lion! Even now they are carrying him in. Behold, in the village they waited many hours for the words of witchdoctor. When he saw how sick the boy was he shrugged his shoulders and said, "There is no medicine that can bring people back from the door of death. It is the will of the ancestors. *Hodu*! The matter is finished!" So they send him to us.'

'Daudi, if it's as bad as all that, you had better prepare the operating room at once and see that everything is ready for a blood transfusion.'

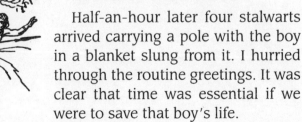

He nodded and hurried off.

Half-an-hour later four stalwarts arrived carrying a pole with the boy in a blanket slung from it. I hurried through the routine greetings. It was clear that time was essential if we were to save that boy's life.

The village Chief stood in front of those carrying the wounded boy. 'Bwana,' he said, 'his name is Mdimi. He is the son of my brother. Behold, was he not looking after the goats of his father when, suddenly, from the tall grasses sprang a lion? With  his paw he slashed at the boy and *yoh*! He fell to the ground as one dead and has been like this ever since.' He pointed with his chin to the unconscious boy.

'The lion did not attack him again?'

'No. He made off with a goat in his mouth and the boy lay there bleeding.'

As I examined him it was painfully clear how shrewd the witchdoctor had been. The boy's shoulder and arm were badly torn and he was extremely shocked.

I looked up. 'We will try to help him, but do not forget that the claws of lions do great damage. Behold, before we can work we will need to give him a blood transfusion.'

The Chief nodded, for he had heard the story of how a life could be saved by the use of living blood.

'Bwana, he is of my family. I shall give him the blood.'

'Good. Daudi will come and do the test.'

Nurses came hurrying with blankets and raised the foot of the bed. Wendwa gave an injection to stop pain.

Suddenly Daudi burst into the room.

'Doctor,' he said, speaking in English, 'this is a matter to fix at once.' I hurried after him.

The Chief had ulcers on his leg that looked as though they had been punched out by a machine. I examined him quickly and shook my head.

'Great One, we cannot use your blood. There is disease in it.'

He started to bluster but I held up my hand, 'Stop. This is no time for words. Daudi, see if there are others who will help the boy. Now I must hurry to the operating table and work. It would have been better to give him the blood first but I must act with speed to save his life. May I leave the transfusion to you?'

In the operating room we worked fast. Above all else time was important. Deftly Wendwa gave me the necessary instruments. The lion's claws had done ugly damage but fortunately no bones were broken nor was anything vital torn.

'Wendwa, I am planning to take away any flesh that is dead, and any pieces of tissue that will never heal or that might contain germs from the claws of the lion. There may be fibres or infection from the blanket in which he was carried or from the dirt and dust from the road. The real danger is not only the wound but the shock.'

The dressings and bandages were soon in place. Mboga carried the boy in his arms and placed him gently in his bed.

Daudi hurried in with a bottle of blood and started the transfusion. It was amazing to see how fast it worked on a boy so perilously close to death. The relations crowded round the window and I could hear their voices as they watched.

'What's he doing?'

'Do you not see?' broke in Nusu's deep voice. 'The child was damaged by the lion and lost much of his blood. He did not have enough within his own body. So the Bwana gives him other blood and he lives. You can see it working.'

There were muttered voices in agreement. '*Hongo*, it is as though life flows from the bottle into him.'

'Truly, that is what is happening.'

'Where did the blood come from?'

Daudi looked over his shoulder saying softly, 'The one who gave the blood is the son of the Great Chief of the whole country.'

'You mean Mapinde's son, Isaka?'

'*Eheh*, doctor. Behold has he not heard the words of God and have they not stayed firmly in his head? Truly, he is one that follows the ways of God. He is indeed a member of God's family, this one.'

I turned to the window. 'Is Isaka there?' There was a movement. Through the door came a tall young man.

'Bwana?' he said.

'They tell me that the blood that is even now saving young Mdimi is yours.'

Isaka smiled. 'Yes, Bwana. It is good that it is the right type.'

'Why did you give it to him, Isaka? Is he a member of your family?'

He nodded. 'He is the child of the cousin of my father's third wife.'

Daudi grinned but Isaka turned to all who were listening. 'It gave me joy to give my blood to him for I would bear witness to the Son of the God of all gods, Jesus Christ. He died so that I could be forgiven and even now I'm sharing in the life that never ends.'

Goha was sitting up in bed. 'I also believe in Jesus and love him.'

'I too,' came Chuma's voice. 'But behold, I am a child in these things. It is only these days that I have joined him and come into his family.'

Isaka smiled all over his face. 'These are important words. Behold, in a few days is it not the time when we rejoice because of his birthday? When I heard of Mdimi here in this great trouble, I prayed and asked the Lord Jesus what he wanted me to do. Then I thought, perhaps my blood will save his ordinary life and then, maybe, he will understand what I have found about Jesus himself.'

'And you gave Jesus a gift which will bring great pleasure to his heart today. It is as though the blood you gave was given to Jesus Christ himself.'

Isaka bowed his head. 'Bwana, this gives me great satisfaction.'

As the last of the transfusion ran into Mdimi's veins his eyelids fluttered

and opened. 'Where am I? What happened? Where is the lion?'

'All is well. The lion is gone. Drink this.'

I gave him some hot, sweet fluid to drink. He swallowed thirstily. After another injection he sank back into sleep.

A crowd of people had come from the village where Mdimi lived. Daudi walked outside and took them to the shade of the pomegranate tree.

'It is a day of rejoicing,' he said. 'A child's life has been saved, a life that many thought was lost. But, behold, he lives.'

I turned to Mboga. 'He lives truly. But the work is not yet finished. He is still sick, sick *kabisa*.'

After a final look at Mdimi, I arranged for Goha's bed to be brought into the same room.

Daudi hurried in and took me by the arm. We walked out under the pepper trees. 'What is the news of Goha?'

'He has much contentment. Is that why you called me so urgently?'

Daudi shook his head. 'Bwana, news has come from Woga's village.' He spat.

When Daudi did that I knew we faced an ugly brand of trouble.

11
Retwist

'You remember the wild drumming we heard the night before last, doctor?'

'Yes.'

'You remember how Woga went home complaining, "I have great thirst"?'

I nodded.

'Before dawn he swallowed two large gourdfuls of beer.'

'*Yoh*, surely few men could do that.'

'He did, for he drank from sundown to dawn.'

'That will produce much trouble. He might as well try to put out a fire with kerosene as improve the condition of his joints by drinking beer.'

Daudi nodded. 'The news is that he is coming to the hospital again with trouble in his mind. His pains are back but his wisdom has gone. I hear that he will arrive when the sun is directly overhead. *Yoh*, and when he comes...!' Daudi shrugged his shoulders.

We walked up the hill to the outpatients' room. People were crowding round and everybody seemed to be speaking at once.

Chuma stood beside me. 'Bwana, I want to sharpen jungle knives.'

'*Eheh*, don't wear out the grindstone.'

Chuma grinned.

Wendwa came up. 'Bwana, here is a small piece of trouble. A basket of flour has been brought in as a gift and it is full of weevils. What will we do with it?'

'Put it here for the time being, Wendwa.'

Small Joy's voice came from the shade of the verandah. 'Bwana, my throat, *oohee*, it is hot inside and dry as a cooking pot. Also inside my throat are two things large as thumbs that choke me. They…'

I knew one certain way to stop a conversation like that. I turned to Daudi. 'Pass me the tongue depressor. Open wide!'

I pushed his tongue down firmly. 'Say *aaah*!' Somehow he wriggled away from the depressor.

'Paint my throat, Bwana,' he croaked. 'Paint it with the medicine the colour of sunset!'

Daudi grinned. 'He means gentian violet, doctor.'

'*Eheh*, we will do that if you wish.'

'Bwana, that's medicine. *Yoh*, it helps.'

Before he could say another word an old man pushed him to one side and grumbled, 'My cough, Bwana, it is as though my ribs were dragged apart. Sometimes it is as though a lion roared. Sometimes, Bwana, it is as though locusts make their strange noise in my head. *Yoh*, I have trouble within me.' He in his turn was pushed aside by an old woman. 'Bwana, my eyes. They burn like coals of fire.'

Over her shoulder came another voice, 'But Bwana, mine are worse than hers. They stick together. Give me medicine.'

Again Small Joy's voice came, 'My throat is better, thanks to the purple medicine, but not my stomach. There is a restless snake within it.'

Goha came rushing round the corner. 'Bwana, quickly, they are fighting.'

'Who are they?'

'Chuma and Woga. They are slashing at each other with knives, Bwana. Somebody will be killed. Quickly!'

I grabbed the basket of flour. Daudi and Nusu ran with me. In front of the men's ward there was an excited crowd. Woga was yelling and waving his *panga* angrily. Chuma stood his ground holding his weapon defensively. He looked quite capable of protecting himself.

Woga shouted harshly, 'I'll cut out your liver, little man. I'll feed it to the crows.'

Swish went his *panga* through the air.

I gave hasty instructions to Daudi. 'You deal with Chuma. Grab him from the back when I've fixed this loud-mouthed Woga. Nusu, stay with me.'

'*Eeeh*,' screeched Woga, stabbing the air, 'on the point of my knife I'll spear your kidneys and chop them into small slices.'

Those who stood round moved back involuntarily.

My gout patient was going on with his butchery process. 'I'll chop your heart and lungs to a size suitable for jackals.'

He swayed a little for he was drunk. It was obvious that he was getting ready to lurch into attack. I grabbed the basket of weevily flour. He moved forwards and leapt. A blinding, choking basket of flour, complete with weevils, caught him in the face. He staggered back, coughing and spluttering.

Daudi's arms went round Chuma and held him firmly. I chopped down with the heel of my hand, hitting Woga's arm right on a nerve. He yelled and dropped the *panga*, his hand numb for the moment. Goha scuttled in to pick up the knife. I twisted Woga's arm behind his back and Nusu held him with a sort of head lock.

Woga roared, 'Mind my toe, my toe, my swollen toe!'

Nusu had taken the knife from Chuma, who was wiping his forehead.

'*Yoh*,' he said, 'I thought one of us would be in small pieces by now. Let me show that beer-soaked, useless one the things he ought to know. His memory will be helped only by bruises. Bwana, at least let me beat him with the flat of the knife.'

Daudi muttered fiercely, 'Be quiet!'

I swung the warrior round. 'Woga, you ought to be ashamed of yourself after all the help we gave you here. You should have shown more wisdom than to drink beer. I warned you it would make your trouble worse. Now you come here waving knives and yelling threats and then begging us to be careful of your toe.'

Woga tried to get the flour out of his eyes and nose and ears. He said nothing.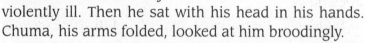

'Bring me two stools. Seat these two men on them and watch them. Also, bring strong coffee.'

Woga struggled to his feet and was suddenly violently ill. Then he sat with his head in his hands. Chuma, his arms folded, looked at him broodingly.

'Bwana, this matter is not finished. It is the custom of our tribe to settle such a thing with spears and with clubs.'

Woga looked across at him with smouldering eyes. '*Yoh*! boastful one, a little spear would drain away much of your pride.'

Mboga stood between them. 'Stop snarling, jackals, or the Bwana will stab you both with little needles and lie you snoring side by side for all to see and laugh at.'

Growls came from both warriors. 'Anger, red eyes and wildly surging blood require small courage,' went on Mboga. 'If you have real courage, prove it, not by cutting each other up for us to patch up later but by doing something to show that you are more than anger surrounded by skin. Do not the members of the Maasai tribe kill a lion to prove their manhood?'

'*Eheh*,' cried Daudi. 'Words of wisdom. Let each of them kill a lion to prove their strength.'

Chuma stood up, his eyes gleaming, but Woga was violently sick again. Chuma sneered, 'Behold, he has fear.'

'This is not fear,' gulped his opponent and made uncomfortable noises.

'But who would have joy in eating a lion?' I asked. 'Ngubi - the wart hog, is as fierce as any lion – also his flesh is joy to the teeth.'

'Roast pig,' chuckled Mboga.

Woga groaned. 'Not with my stomach feeling as it does now.'

Suddenly there was laughter and the tension eased.

'*Eheh*,' said Daudi. 'Let each man take a spear and one go to the east and one to the west and at nightfall he who returns with the fullest hands shall be the stronger.'

Woga stood up shaking. 'I am in no shape to hunt an animal.'

'Why didn't you think of that when you started out in anger to come here and when you decided to wave *pangas* about and slice Chuma in pieces?'

'My head was full of small wisdom, Bwana, because my toe swelled and pain gnawed with cruel teeth.'

'*Eheh*, your toe was full of fire because your stomach was full of beer. You have large muscles and big bones, but surely you have small wisdom.'

Woga groaned and caressed his swollen toes. 'Bwana, give me pills today and tomorrow I'll hunt and bring *Nhembo* - the elephant himself, back on my shoulders.'

Chuma smiled. 'Words, and words and words.'

'Bwana,' came a voice behind me. 'My eyes burn like coals of fire. Give me medicine.'

'*Eheh*, Bwana. What about my stomach, my restless snake?'

'Behold, I'll give you medicine. But first, Daudi, give this medicine to Woga.'

When he came back he chuckled. 'Old Small Joy is in difficulties these days.'

'*Hongo*! I thought he looked much better.'

'His difficulty is finding things that are wrong with him. His tongue is no longer swollen, the thing in his throat that he could neither swallow nor cough up just isn't there, his stomach has peace and the restless snakes have gone on safari.'

'Does the liver still fight with the spleen?'

Daudi laughed. 'Not since we gave him medicine for his malaria, doctor.'

Later that morning Goha came to see me. 'Bwana, the mould is also coming off the old man's soul. He listens to the word of God and has interest in it. I talked to him about donkeys, how Jesus' mother rode one the day before he was born, how he was carried as a small boy to Egypt when King Herod had no joy in hearing of the Son of God coming into the world. I also told him the heartbreaking story of what Jesus allowed men to do to him to overcome the crookedness of our souls. He listens. He is one in whom understanding grows slowly. Again and again I have said the words of Jesus himself so that he will not forget them, so that they will be woven into his memory.'

'What were the words, Goha?'

'The ones you taught me, Bwana. "Come unto me and I will give you rest. Come all who are weary and heavy-laden and I will give you rest. Learn about me and you will find rest for your souls."'

'That's good. But, Goha, make sure that he understands that it isn't enough merely to know about God.'

'*Eheh*, Bwana. I told him it wasn't enough just to know that there was a hospital on the hill, he had to come here and taste the medicines before he could get rid of the troubles of his inside.'

'Do you think he is understanding?'.

Daudi had come up at that moment. He nodded his head. '*Eheh*, doctor, many of us have helped. He will understand. Truly, he will have to change his name from Small Joy before long.'

12
Broken Neck

'Bwana, quickly, come at once.'

I yawned. I'd been up all night working in the hospital. 'What's happening now?'

'Bwana, our friend of many days, the hunter Baruti, is in danger. Come quickly in the car with your rifle.'

'But what has happened?'

'Before dawn the lion that wounded the boy Mdimi came again to the village. Baruti stalked it but the moon gave too little light. He struck with bad aim, wounding but not killing. Now he is up a tree without weapons and the lion is below full of rage. Come quickly, Bwana, and shoot him.'

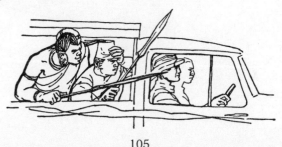

'*Yoh*! My rifle is such that it would do little more than bend his hide. It is useful for shooting rats and snakes, but lions…'

Chuma and Nusu were among those who came running towards us. They heard the story. Chuma stepped forward. 'Bwana, let me kill the creature.'

Nusu was at his side. 'Bwana, rather let us kill that lion.'

The two men chose their spears carefully. Everybody scrambled into old Sukuma, the truck, and we drove to a place where we could watch the drama. I felt useless with only a pea rifle and a *panga*. We drove up the side of the hill and then coasted to a stop. A handful of paces away on the limb of a buyu tree squatted Baruti. From beneath him came blood-curdling snarling.

Lions can certainly climb trees, but Baruti had carefully taken up his position on a limb hard for any lion to reach.

Nusu and Chuma talked earnestly together for a moment and then, taking care that the wind was coming into their faces, they moved stealthily forward through the dry grass. Chuma moved in from the east and Nusu from the north.

Baruti did his best to hold the attention of the lion. Intently we watched the movement of the two hunters. They were creeping closer but were too far away to strike. They would have to move silently at least another fifty metres.

It seemed that at any moment one or other of the hunters would leap to his feet and rush in with his spear but then, dramatically, Woga, very drunk, came staggering into view.

He strode towards the lion and roared at the top of his voice, 'Just what I'm looking for. A lion. Come here to me, noisy one, and I, the beer drinker, will tear your tongue out with my bare hands.'

The lion roared and turned his left side on to Chuma. Here was a chance to drive the spear behind the creature's shoulder into its heart.

Chuma leapt forward, spear raised, then he stumbled. The spear gashed the lion's shoulder but did little harm. The huge tawny animal, teeth bared, turned on him.

Nusu came rushing in and drove his spear at the menacing throat. To my horror, the haft snapped off in his hand.

The lion sprang at the fallen figure of Chuma. It seemed that nothing could save him. Then, from the limb high above, Baruti leapt. His rigid heels landed on the neck of the great beast as it was in the air. Even

at a distance I heard the sharp crack of the lion's neck bones as it fell dead and quivering within a pace of Chuma. He struggled to his feet, grabbed his fallen spear and drove it into the heart of the already dead animal.

We rushed down the hill. In the village, drums throbbed and triumphant singing started up. Woga staggered into a large spiky cactus. He sat stupidly in the middle of it, muttering.

Nusu gripped Baruti's hand. '*Kumbe*, both that ungrateful one and I would have been dead but for you. What man in the whole jungle has ever before killed a lion with his bare feet?'

Baruti shrugged. 'I merely jumped to give Chuma time to stand up again. It was a thing of good fortune that I hit that lion's neck!'

By now the people from the village had come by the score. The drums and the singing were deafening. I held up both my hands for silence.

'Listen, everybody. Tonight will be a night of rejoicing at the hospital. Come all of you and sing'

'*Asante*, Bwana, thank you. We will come with joy.'

Chuma started to skin the lion and Baruti came to me. 'Bwana, my feet, they are bruised I think.'

He sat on the ground. I ran my finger over his skin. One of the bones of his left leg was broken.

'We will fix this at the hospital. It is the fibula, not the main bone of your leg, that is broken. We will put it in plaster.'

Out of the corner of my eye I noticed Chuma walking off into the jungle with a spear over his shoulder.

Fortunately, Baruti's broken bone was in good position and it was only a matter of putting a supporting plaster in place.

He grinned. '*Yoh*, Bwana, that feels better at once.'

We watched Woga disappear among the distant baobab trees.

I groaned. 'Look at that. He chooses to walk into trouble with his eyes open.'

13

Untangling Plans

'What news of Baruti, Daudi?'

'He has much laughter. He is getting many people to write their names on his plaster. But, doctor, it is Chuma that I want to tell you about.'

'What has he been up to?'

'He went hunting. He has brought back to the hospital a large pig. We will roast it tonight and sing around the fire. Will you come?'

'Oh, yes, I'll come. The programme sounds good to me. By the way, young Goha seems happy today.'

'*Eheh*, Bwana, but deep inside him is fear of the operation we plan to do on his face.'

'But Nusu has helped him. Seeing someone who travelled the same path safely before him would...'

'*Eheh*, but while he wishes above all things for it to be done, he still has fear.'

'The last operation upset him a great deal, I know, Daudi.'

'Truly. I was talking to him on the evening that young Mdimi was brought in so badly injured by the lion. He told me that he had a great hope but, doctor, it is too late for that now.'

'*Ooh*, what was that, Daudi?'

'No good talking about that now, doctor, it is too late. Tomorrow's Christmas.'

'Yes, I know that but what was his great hope? Tell me, Daudi. Don't keep me in suspense.'

'Doctor, I don't think it is proper for me to tell you.'

'Why?'

'Goha wouldn't like it.'

'Let me ask you another question, Daudi. What would bring the greatest happiness to the boy?'

Daudi grinned. '*Kah*, doctor, that's different. I can answer that. He longs to wake up on Christmas Day with an ordinary face, one without twists, and he wants the change to happen without him thinking of the operation, without fear or pain.'

I looked at my watch. It was four o'clock in the afternoon.

'It's the tenth hour of the day, Daudi.'

Was that too late to plan something? Ideas surged through my mind. It could be done. I turned to Daudi.

'Prepare the operating theatre. I'll work tonight but it must be secret. We will do something unusual and special tonight. What a Christmas eve this is going to be!'

'How are we to operate without upsetting him, doctor?'

'We'll have to arrange every detail with special care. Your first job is to set out the instruments we'll need.'

Daudi nodded and hurried out of the room. If we were to operate, Goha must have no evening meal. How was I to fix this without making him suspicious?

Chuma was walking past. I beckoned. 'Blacksmith, I want your help in a matter which needs a tongue that can both be still and also skilfully active.'

Chuma lifted one eyebrow and nodded.

'Go to young Goha and say you have a secret plan for the late evening. The sort of secret in which it is most important not to eat the ordinary food at sunset and especially to eat none of the pig you killed with your spear.'

'*Kumbe*, Bwana, what is happening – a special feast?' From my pocket emerged a bottle of many-coloured jelly beans. 'Know what these are?'

'*Eheh*, Bwana. Sugar beans that bring joy to stomachs.'

'Do you think you could swallow one whole?'

'I don't know. I can try, but *yoh*! They're big!'

'Will you have a competition with Goha and some others? The yellow ones are for him and the red ones for you. For my plan to work, Goha must swallow his jelly bean whole, for in it I shall put sleep medicine.'

Chuma rolled his eyes and smiled.

'*Kumbe*! I begin to see your cunning. *Yoh*! Bwana, I will help.'

'Plan things out so that all may go smoothly. Leave the rest to me.'

'I shall do it, Bwana.'

I went into my office and unlocked the cupboard which contained the powerful drugs. From a bottle came a canary-coloured capsule. I slit open a yellow jelly bean, scooped out some of the glucose, fitted the capsule into place and repaired the bean-shaped sweet. In it were enough drugs to make Goha fall asleep in twenty minutes.

From a folder I took out a number of medical diagrams and anatomy drawings of the face. The operation was complicated. Underneath the boy's eye, deep in, was a tumour the size of a large spider. It was as though the legs reached out and deliberately dragged the eyelid out of place, twisting the corner of his mouth and puckering up his lip and nostril. This had been there since birth and distorted his face. The deformity could be corrected by a piece of delicate surgery. I asked God to help me to work with sufficient skill to remove the ugliness once and for all.

Again I checked the stages of the operation and the exact position of nerves and arteries. I drew a couple of special diagrams and stuck them onto the window to guide me if anything unusual cropped up.

Every lamp in the hospital was alight. The whole place was being decorated and laughing voices seemed to come from all directions.

I went across to the men's ward. Mdimi, still heavily bandaged, was clutching the side of his bed with his good arm and laughing. 'Blow up that balloon. Blow with strength!'

Chuma blew powerfully with his cheeks bulging.

'More?'

'More and more,' urged Goha.

The blacksmith filled his broad chest and blew. The balloon was incredibly large.

POP!

'*Yoh*!' Goha's expression was one of excitement. 'Behold, it's gone! Nothing remains but a little bit of red stuff.'

Baruti limped in with an armful of decorations while Wendwa carefully looped around the wall streamers of coloured paper and sparkling dangling balls that made the windows seem to come alive and twinkle.

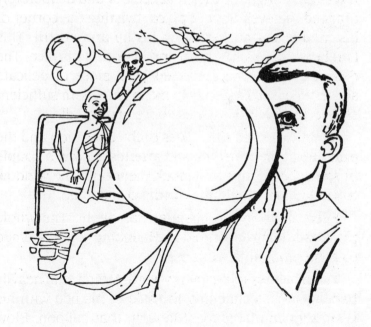

I took Mdimi's pulse. It was regular. 'How is the shoulder and the arm?'

'Stiff, Bwana, but not sore unless I move it. But *yoh*…'

He gazed wide-eyed as Daudi staggered in with a pepper tree limb in a kerosene tin. It was decorated with tinsel and pink cotton wool. The boy's eyes took in everything in the small ward.

'Christmas isn't merely a time to decorate and sing and give presents and receive gifts, is it, Bwana?'

'No, Mdimi, it's the birthday of the Son of God himself. We think especially of him at Christmas.'

His eyes seemed to be looking away out in the distance. Suddenly he spoke. 'Jesus is wonderful doing all this for us. But I have sadness.'

'Why?'

'It is his great day and I have nothing to offer him, no gift of any sort and I greatly want to give him something he'd like best of all.'

'There is such a thing, Mdimi, and it is here for the giving.'

He sat bolt upright and flinched as pain came from his torn shoulder.

'What is it, Bwana?'

'King Daudi told us in *Zaburi* - the Psalms. He asks the question, "What shall I give back to God for all his great gifts to me?" Then he answers it, "I will

116

take the cup of salvation and praise the name of the Lord." You ask him to set you free from your sin and he gives you a share in the victory he came to earth to win, and you give yourself to him. Listen, they sing it even now.'

In the doorway I could see Chuma listening intently. The words came, 'Just as I am without one plea, but that your blood was shed for me, and that you say, "Come to me," Oh, Lamb of God, I come.'

'Yes, Jesus, I come,' whispered Mdimi.

Through the doorway I saw Chuma nodding his head in complete agreement.

Goha sat quietly on his bed. 'Do you really mean that deep down?'

Mdimi nodded.

'Then you have given Jesus what he came to earth for, and what he died to do. The Bible says that there is happiness in heaven when people come to God.'

Outside Daudi had put on a record. The warm African night was full of harp music and then the braying of a donkey and the lowing of cattle.

Bethlehem seemed very close.

14
Near to Bethlehem

Daudi came over to me. 'All is ready, doctor.'

He pointed with his chin to a blazing fire. Round it were an excited group, most of them singing, although a number of small boys were more interested in the pig which was being roasted.

'There will much singing tonight,' said Daudi.

'They can rejoice while we work in the operating theatre.'

He smiled. 'What sort of anaesthetic will you use?'

I held up the jelly beans. They looked most colourful in the large bottle. Then I showed him the yellow one. 'This jelly bean is loaded with sleep medicine. We'll trick Goha into swallowing it and he'll be asleep in twenty minutes, then an injection will carry on the good work. We can't risk shock.'

'That is a way of wisdom, doctor.'

The singing started in earnest at that moment. Chuma and Nusu were singing a variety of African duets with everybody joining in the chorus. As they finished I stepped forward.

'*Yoh*, that is real singing!'

Daudi nodded his head. 'It is true food for the ears.'

'Talking of food,' I stood up and tipped some jelly beans into my hand, 'here is a competition. Who can swallow one of these at a gulp?'

'*Yoh*,' Chuma scrambled to his feet. 'I challenge Baruti to a swallowing contest.'

'That's fair.' I held up the bottle. 'Six beans of sugar to the winner. Come on.'

Chuma opened his mouth wide. I placed a red jelly bean on his tongue and told him to swallow. He rolled his eyeballs, tears ran out of them as he struggled to swallow and then coughed and spluttered. The crowd rocked with laughter.

'*Yoh*,' he gasped. 'You need to be Ostrich himself to swallow one of those.'

'Open your mouth wide,' said Goha, 'and then I can see you are not cheating.'

Chuma opened his mouth and there was the jelly bean underneath his tongue.

'Spit it out, you cheat,' shouted Goha. 'Bwana, give him no more.'

'*Yoh*,' grinned the blacksmith. 'I can't swallow these things.'

'I can,' said Goha.

I produced the yellow jelly bean.

'Open your mouth wide, Goha. I'll tell you how

to do it. Chuma didn't put it far enough back on his tongue.'

Goha's tongue came out a surprising distance. Far back on it I placed the yellow jelly bean. He swallowed. It was gone.

A smile came over his face. '*Yoh*, Bwana. It is on its way.' He stretched out his hand.

'*Eeeh*,' boomed Chuma. 'Open your mouth, Small One, that I might see if it has gone.'

It was painfully obvious when Goha tried to do so that his mouth was twisted out of shape. I tried to cover his embarrassment by spilling the beans.

Baruti picked up a handful, stuck out a huge tongue, decorated it with six of the sugar beans and swallowed the lot, throwing his head back.

'*Yooh*!' roared Chuma. 'There was sight to bring envy to the heart of Kiboko - the hippo, himself.'

Baruti was suddenly serious. '*Kumbe*! I have been thinking this afternoon. It is easy to think when your leg is in plaster. It is easy to rejoice when you are in safety, when your nose is tickled by the accompanying smell of roast pig. But only this morning there was danger lurking in the village. Not long ago Mdimi here came close to the gate of death when the lion attacked him. I, too, came close when I threw my spear with small skill. But now the lion is dead and we rejoice.

'Let us not forget, however, that among us there is a thing with stronger teeth than lions and sharper claws. It is not the everyday habit of lions to hunt men to kill them, but the thing that I speak of with wicked teeth and wicked claws constantly looks for men to kill, to make them miserable, to bring unhappiness. It is the beast called "Sin".

'Between us we killed the lion this morning, but all men put together can do nothing to sin. Only the Great Chief himself, the God of gods, can deal with this beast. In conquering it he was wounded and he died, but he lives because he is God Almighty. We have thankfulness because the lion is dead. We pat one another on the shoulders because of the killing of it. Should we not have special thankfulness also to God for what he has done in conquering this beast? Do not many of us have a greater happiness in our hearts which is deeper than all ordinary feelings? Let us think of these things as we feast tonight.'

Beside me Goha's head was nodding. He yawned. His voice was a whisper. '*Yoh*, Bwana, I'm tired.'

Chuma came across and picked him up in strong arms. Hardly anyone noticed us move over to the ward. As he put the boy gently down in his bed Chuma smiled at me. 'Well, Bwana, that was the first stage of his Christmas present.'

15
Christmas Gift

Outside the singing continued enthusiastically. Inside the operating theatre we bowed our heads and prayed.

'O God, your hand on mine, please, that the crooked places may be made straight for this boy. Lord, he loves you. Please help me to help him in a way which will mean so much to him.'

I pulled on my gloves and started.

'How long will it take, doctor?'

'Perhaps two hours.'

Before long the tumour was exposed. It looked more like an octopus than a spider. Its fibrous tentacles seemed to drag structures out of place, twisting the skin, distorting the tissues. With considerable caution, I dissected. An hour had gone when I reached the last ugly tentacle. It looked complicated but came away with little difficulty. Its removal could easily have damaged the eye. I let out a sigh of relief.

'*Hongo*, Daudi, I am glad that's over.'

'Now, doctor,' urged Wendwa, 'stitch with skill so that the scar will not show.'

I smiled. 'That's all very well for you, a woman, but I am only a man. However I will do my best.'

But my sewing was not satisfactory to her.

She peered closely at my work. 'Doctor, see here, it puckers a little!'

I took out the stitch and put in a new one.

'That's better, but the next stitch...I think you should do that one again.'

I did so. She looked at it carefully.

'*Eheh*, Bwana, that's better. For a man that's good.'

It was with relief that we smiled at each other over our masks as I placed a wisp of sterile cotton wool over the stitching and then added a few drops of Friar's Balsam. The dressing blended with Goha's chocolate-coloured skin.

I was about to take off my gloves when Daudi said, 'Doctor, what an opportunity to take away the other tumour!'

Thoughtfully I replied, 'You are right, Daudi. We have everything ready. He's showing no signs of shock.'

Wendwa nodded.

'Well, boil up all the instruments, Daudi.'

'They are all ready for you, doctor. I hoped we could do this.'

I felt a twinge of worry as memories of the other tumour ran through my mind, but it was only a matter of minutes before this one was safely removed and the skin stitched smoothly.

Daudi looked at me and grinned happily. 'Who'd have thought it could possibly be as easy as that?'

Wendwa looked up from putting on the dressing. 'We prayed, Bwana, remember.'

'*Yoh*,' said Daudi. 'Bwana, look at his face now. What a difference!'

Goha was indeed a good-looking boy. Daudi carried him carefully back to the ward and Wendwa tucked him in.

Daudi said, 'Surely the hand of God was on yours tonight, doctor. That is a work that does not leave its footprints behind it.'

It was midnight as I walked down from the hospital to my house. Enthusiastic carol singers were in full voice. 'Christians awake, salute the happy morn'!

Thought I with weariness, 'Not on your life. I am going to bed. The dawn will come soon enough.'

It came all too quickly.

Mboga's voice from outside woke me. 'Bwana, it is time to come up. They will wake early, these children.'

I dressed quickly. There was a tinge of pink in the east as Daudi, Baruti, Chuma and I went through the hospital gate. We stood silently inside the ward behind a screen so that we could not be seen. Mdimi woke first. At the end of his bed was a colourful cotton bag containing little Christmas gifts.

'*Yoh*,' he cried. 'It's for me. It is Christmas. A gift for me!'

Goha stretched, yawned and woke. The light was growing stronger. Nusu came through the door. 'What have you at the end of your bed?'

Goha sat up. '*Yoh*, there is a big thing there.'

The sun rises fast in our part of Africa. Even as he looked the light became strong enough to see.

'It's a mirror, a large mirror.' He reached out and peered into it.

'What is it?' called Mdimi.

Goha made no attempt to answer. In growing excitement he shouted, 'It's my face, but it's different. The thing that made my face twist is gone, it's gone! I'm straight, I'm straight!'

Tears ran down his cheeks.

There was a scratching at the door. Goha tried to struggle out of bed. His hand went to his chest which suddenly stabbed with pain. He fingered the dressing and nodded his head slowly. Carefully he went to the door and opened it. In leapt the small dog, jumping over his master. Goha's legs started to wobble. He eased himself back between the sheets. The small dog whined and put his paws on the side of the bed.

'Look, Seko. Look!' They both peered into the mirror. The small dog barked. I nudged Daudi with my elbow and we all walked into the room. 'Happy Christmas, Goha. Happy Christmas, Mdimi.'

'Bwana, Bwana, look at my face. It's straight!'

He looked into the mirror most carefully and a smile spread over his face.

'*Yoh*, it is hard to believe what I see. You did it so well, Bwana. Thank you very, very much.'

His new smile matched Nusu's and it was wonderful to see.

The words bubbled out of him. 'Truly, I had no fear! I didn't know a thing of what happened, not a single thing. *Hongo*! And I thought this could not possibly happen!'

His eyes sparkled as his gaze fell on a brand new *ilimba* which Chuma had made and placed at the end of the bed. He touched the instrument lovingly. '*Hongo*, my joy is great,' he said with a catch in his voice.

We tiptoed outside. Mboga's face was glowing. He put a hand on both Daudi's and Chuma's shoulders and smiled broadly at me. '*Kah*! Is it not worthwhile work – to help make crooked things straight?'

SAMPLE CHAPTER FROM:
JUNGLE DOCTOR
and the Whirlwind

1
Bhang!

'That's *bhang*, hash-hish!' Mboga shouted to make himself heard above the clatter of the railway yard. 'It's an evil medicine that makes some people as mad as a charging rhino and others too stupid to move off an ants' nest.'

We were standing near the railway station at Dodoma in Tanzania along a path that was some twenty paces from the metre-gauge track which led from the East African coast to the Great Lakes. A large African police sergeant marched a gaudily dressed young man of the local tribe. The prisoner was frothing at the mouth and yelling at the top of his voice.

The whistle of a goods train sounded long and shrill. The policeman glanced over his shoulder and in that second was tripped by the frenzied man who dragged his arm free and dashed across the rails almost under the wheels of the engine.

The driver yelled, '*Mpumbafu nye!* You stupid muddlehead!'

The irate sergeant stood with his hands on his hips. To attempt to follow was hopeless. There were thirty trucks in that train and by the time the guard's van had passed, his prisoner was lost in the crowded streets.

We walked across the shaded avenue of trees. The sergeant shook his head. 'Behold, he nearly became food for vultures and hyaenas. Many are using this marijuana these days. We will certainly catch him again, but he can do all sorts of damage in the meantime.'

'Is it not possible to destroy the gardens of those who grow this Indian hemp plant?' I asked.

The big policeman shrugged his shoulders. 'To grow it is not forbidden by the law.'

'*Kah!*' grinned Mboga. 'So he and those like him smoke their cigarettes, snuff their snuff, lose their wisdom and give much trouble to you and to the other *askaris.*'

The sergeant nodded. 'And they can bring difficult

work to you at the hospital. Are you on safari, Bwana doctor?'

'Yes, and we're nearly finished. We're visiting small hospitals, giving out medicine in villages way out in the bush and finding those who need to come into hospital for operations on their eyes.'

'And your helper is this man of many words, Mboga?' I nodded. 'Travel with special care. There is trouble about these days since they prepare to grow many peanuts in the fertile country below the hills near Kongwa.'

'What kind of trouble, Bwana sergeant?'

He shook his head. 'Many who are *fundis* - experts - at taking what isn't their own are about. They come from all over the land and even from Kenya. They will steal anything they think they can sell - even the wheels from your car.'

Mboga laughed. 'There is small profit in the wheels of Sukuma.'

I explained. '*Sukuma* in Swahili means "push" and that is the best way to start her. See, is she not waiting for us on a slope?'

'*Heeeh.*' Mboga's eyes twinkled. 'This we find the easiest way to wake her from sleep.'

As we opened the doors of the veteran Ford the *askari* saluted. '*Kwaheri* - goodbye - may your safari be successful.'

Sukuma coughed and sputtered and then moved sedately away from the township. We shuddered our way along the corrugated gravel road leaving behind us a cloud of fine dust.

Soon we were driving through thorn bush country dotted every now and then with small hills of piled-up granite boulders. In places there were patches of dried stalks of maize and millet.

Mboga pointed with his chin. 'Where the soil is good they plant. These last two years the rains have been good. They started in November and went through to March. The harvest was excellent. This year I fear it will be different. I fear for the peanut planters.'

Lorry after lorry came towards us almost smothering us with red, powdery dust. '*Kumbe*! They pay much money to those who drive trucks these days.' A wistful note came into Mboga's voice. 'I wish I had much money, but a second-year male nurse receives few shillings for much work.'

I changed from Swahili into English. 'Listen Spinach, it is a wise saying that enough is enough.'

He nodded and went on in Swahili. 'I understand you, but many think your words have small value and that your proverb is of the same sort. At the peanut growing there is money for those who want it and have cunning in their heads. *Kumbe*! There are many who love money.' He paused and spoke slowly and with emphasis, 'And I am one of them.'

We drove along in silence for a while. I avoided the larger potholes and accelerated when we came to a long downhill stretch. With Sukuma going as fast as she knew how, we jolted less and entered into a patch of thornbush jungle. 'Tell me, Spinach, is this a piece of country where there are rhinos?'

He nodded vigorously. 'And there are those that trap them in a way that would bring you no joy. They make a big loop in a strong piece of wire and put it along the paths that the great animals travel to a water hole. *Kifaru* blunders along and pokes his head into the loop.' Mboga turned towards me and acted out the scene. 'It tightens. He struggles. It cuts into him. He battles. He runs this way. He runs this way, he runs that way and the wire cuts in deeper and deeper. He is frantic with pain but all his efforts are useless. Perhaps for a day or longer he struggles and then he dies. Then comes the trapper, hacks the great horn from the bridge of the dead beast's nose and sells it to one of the traders and makes much money.'

'And the trader makes a lot more money, I suppose. But what of the rhino?'

'Food for hyaenas and vultures and thousands of flies and ants.'

'How would you like to be caught in a trap like that, Mboga?'

He shook his head. 'It is a thing of no joy.'

'You mean to say that if you saw a trap you would not walk into it?'

He laughed. 'Do you think I'm stupid, Bwana doctor?'

'I hope not. *Kah*! How I hope not.'

We turned off from the main road and drove between great grey boulders over a wide stretch of red earth. Occasional cactuses stuck out their spikes. Crows flew overhead to roost in a grove of baobab trees. Abruptly the wheel was almost wrenched from my hands. We skidded wildly and pulled up against a thorn tree, its limbs weighed down with weaver-birds' nests.

Mboga sighed. 'There is small joy in punctures. Let us mend this one with speed and skill or there will be no answer for the famine that calls within me.' He used a trick he had learned from Samson, our hospital strong man, and lifted the whole of the left side of the car off the ground while I slipped the jack into place. He grunted and started to unscrew the punctured wheel.

I lay at full length under the old box-bodied Ford. I could see Tanzania from an unusual angle. In front lay the apology for a road. Framed between the front wheels was a typical picture of the thornbush savanna country: a squat Gogo house - mud-and-wattle walled with a bundle of grass and some pumpkins on the flat roof, and beyond it a boy armed with a knobbed stick was driving a few hungry-looking hump-backed cattle and an assortment of goats and fat-tailed sheep.

Mboga levered off the tyre, blew up the punctured tube and placed it on a patch of dust. A small crater in the dust showed us where the puncture was. He marked it quickly and ran his hand round inside the tyre cover. Using an old pair of dental forceps he drew out a five-centimetre long thorn. Ten minutes later we were on safari again. Mboga was handling the thorn thoughtfully.

'It's hard, sharp, difficult to see, and the cause of all our trouble.'

I nodded. 'In a way it's a trap too.'

'Trap?' questioned Mboga. 'You're talking a lot about traps this afternoon.'

'You started it. You said, "I wish I had much money. I love money".'

'Well, why not, Bwana? If you have money you can buy things.'

'Spinach, my friend, you do not understand. Would Rhino have put his head into the noose if he'd seen it? Would I have driven over that thorn if I had seen it sticking up in the dust? This is the cunning of traps. Animals and people don't realise they're there.'

'*Yoh*, when you call me Spinach I know you have something you want me to remember.'

137

'It's what you name means in English and I like the sound of it.'

We drove over a dry riverbed and up the steep bank on the far side. Ahead of us was a hospital where we would work for a few days. People ran out to greet us.

'Make sure you deal properly with your famine,' I laughed, 'for we will be busy tomorrow. I will have many injections to give and you will have the chance to show your skill in bandaging. Oh, and Mboga, would you see if Elisha has finished his building? Ask him to be ready to return with us in two days' time.'

Jungle Doctor Series

Adventures with a Mission Flavour

African Adventures by Dick Anderson
ISBN 978-1-85792-807-5

Amazon Adventures by Horace Banner
ISBN 978-1-85792-440-4

Great Barrier Reef Adventures by Jim Cromarty
ISBN 978-1-84550-068-9

Himalayan Adventures by Penny Reeve
ISBN 978-1-84550-080-1

Kiwi Adventures
ISBN 978-1-84550-282-9

Outback Adventures by Jim Cromarty
ISBN 978-185792-974-4

Rainforest Adventures by Horace Banner
ISBN 978-185792-627-9

Rocky Mountain Adventures by Betty Swinford
ISBN 978-1-85792-962-1

Scottish Highland Adventures by Catherine Mackenzie
ISBN 978-1-84550-281-2

Wild West Adventures by Donna Vann
ISBN 978-1-84550-065-8

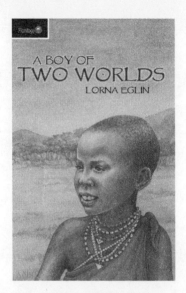

A Boy of Two Worlds by Lorna Eglin
ISBN 978-1-84550-126-6

Maasai boys love to practice throwing spears, and jumping. One day they will be strong men and leaders of their tribe. Lemayan is excellent with the goats and his father is proud of his capable son.

One dreadful day all that changes and the tribe's way of life hangs in the balance; the drought attacks their pastures; worms attack the cattle and the whole tribe has to sell all their animals. To make matters worse Lemayan falls sick - but no one realises just how sick.

Lemayan only knows the traditional Maasai world... but now he has to live in a different world. What will that different world offer him? Will he be happy? Will anything be as good as looking after animals?

When Lemayan finds out about a Good Shepherd who cares for his sheep he begins another journey of discovery... a journey to yet another world ... a world where the Lord Jesus is King... and where all tribes and peoples are welcome.

CHRISTIAN FOCUS PUBLICATIONS

Christian Focus Christian Heritage CF4K Mentor

Christian Focus Publications publishes books for adults and children under its four main imprints: Christian Focus, CF4K, Mentor and Christian Heritage. Our books reflect that God's word is reliable and Jesus is the way to know him, and live for ever with him.

Our children's publication list includes a Sunday School curriculum that covers pre-school to early teens; puzzle and activity books. We also publish personal and family devotional titles, biographies and inspirational stories that children will love.

If you are looking for quality Bible teaching for children then we have an excellent range of Bible story and age specific theological books.

From pre-school to teenage fiction, we have it covered!

**Find us at our web page:
www.christianfocus.com**